NUCLEAR DEAL FALLOUT:
THE GLOBAL THREAT OF IRAN

HEARING

BEFORE THE

SUBCOMMITTEE ON TERRORISM, NONPROLIFERATION, AND TRADE

OF THE

COMMITTEE ON FOREIGN AFFAIRS
HOUSE OF REPRESENTATIVES

ONE HUNDRED FIFTEENTH CONGRESS

FIRST SESSION

MAY 24, 2017

Serial No. 115–28

Printed for the use of the Committee on Foreign Affairs

Available via the World Wide Web: http://www.foreignaffairs.house.gov/ or
http://www.gpo.gov/fdsys/

U.S. GOVERNMENT PUBLISHING OFFICE

25–556PDF   WASHINGTON : 2017

For sale by the Superintendent of Documents, U.S. Government Publishing Office
Internet: bookstore.gpo.gov   Phone: toll free (866) 512–1800; DC area (202) 512–1800
Fax: (202) 512–2104   Mail: Stop IDCC, Washington, DC 20402–0001

COMMITTEE ON FOREIGN AFFAIRS

EDWARD R. ROYCE, California, *Chairman*

CHRISTOPHER H. SMITH, New Jersey
ILEANA ROS-LEHTINEN, Florida
DANA ROHRABACHER, California
STEVE CHABOT, Ohio
JOE WILSON, South Carolina
MICHAEL T. McCAUL, Texas
TED POE, Texas
DARRELL E. ISSA, California
TOM MARINO, Pennsylvania
JEFF DUNCAN, South Carolina
MO BROOKS, Alabama
PAUL COOK, California
SCOTT PERRY, Pennsylvania
RON DeSANTIS, Florida
MARK MEADOWS, North Carolina
TED S. YOHO, Florida
ADAM KINZINGER, Illinois
LEE M. ZELDIN, New York
DANIEL M. DONOVAN, JR., New York
F. JAMES SENSENBRENNER, JR.,
  Wisconsin
ANN WAGNER, Missouri
BRIAN J. MAST, Florida
FRANCIS ROONEY, Florida
BRIAN K. FITZPATRICK, Pennsylvania
THOMAS A. GARRETT, JR., Virginia

ELIOT L. ENGEL, New York
BRAD SHERMAN, California
GREGORY W. MEEKS, New York
ALBIO SIRES, New Jersey
GERALD E. CONNOLLY, Virginia
THEODORE E. DEUTCH, Florida
KAREN BASS, California
WILLIAM R. KEATING, Massachusetts
DAVID N. CICILLINE, Rhode Island
AMI BERA, California
LOIS FRANKEL, Florida
TULSI GABBARD, Hawaii
JOAQUIN CASTRO, Texas
ROBIN L. KELLY, Illinois
BRENDAN F. BOYLE, Pennsylvania
DINA TITUS, Nevada
NORMA J. TORRES, California
BRADLEY SCOTT SCHNEIDER, Illinois
THOMAS R. SUOZZI, New York
ADRIANO ESPAILLAT, New York
TED LIEU, California

AMY PORTER, *Chief of Staff*   THOMAS SHEEHY, *Staff Director*
JASON STEINBAUM, *Democratic Staff Director*

————

SUBCOMMITTEE ON TERRORISM, NONPROLIFERATION, AND TRADE

TED POE, Texas, *Chairman*

JOE WILSON, South Carolina
DARRELL E. ISSA, California
PAUL COOK, California
SCOTT PERRY, Pennsylvania
LEE M. ZELDIN, New York
BRIAN J. MAST, Florida
THOMAS A. GARRETT, JR., Virginia

WILLIAM R. KEATING, Massachusetts
LOIS FRANKEL, Florida
BRENDAN F. BOYLE, Pennsylvania
DINA TITUS, Nevada
NORMA J. TORRES, California
BRADLEY SCOTT SCHNEIDER, Illinois

(II)

CONTENTS

NUCLEAR DEAL FALLOUT: THE GLOBAL THREAT OF IRAN

WEDNESDAY, MAY 24, 2017

House of Representatives,
Subcommittee on Terrorism, Nonproliferation, and Trade,
Committee on Foreign Affairs,
Washington, DC.

The subcommittee met, pursuant to notice, at 2:09 p.m., in room 2172, Rayburn House Office Building, Hon. Ted Poe (chairman of the subcommittee) presiding.

Mr. POE. The subcommittee will come to order.

Without objection, all members may have 5 days to submit statements, questions, extraneous materials for the record, subject to the length limitation and the rules.

I will make my opening statement.

Two years ago, Iran and six major world powers reached an agreement regarding its program of nuclear capability. That deal was a result of a decade of tough U.S. and international sanctions placed on the Iranian regime because of its dangerous nuclear ambitions.

The mullahs in Tehran felt the pain of sanctions. That is why they came to the negotiating table. At that moment, we had the most leverage over the regime. But, unfortunately, a deal that the past administration brokered turns out to be seriously flawed.

For starters, the deal simply put Iran's nuclear plans on hold for 10 to 15 years. After that time, Iran is free to develop a nuclear weapon and menace the world. Even worse, the deal did not address Iran's continued sponsorship of terrorists with American blood on their hands. It also did nothing to curb the development of ballistic missiles.

Iran gained immediate access to hundreds of billions of dollars, and the promise of yet more to come, due to the sanctions' relief. Only weeks after the announcement of the deal, reports indicated that Iran had significantly increased funding to Hezbollah and Hamas, both terrorist groups. This increased funding allowed Hezbollah to increase its operations in Syria, where the group has deepened its sectarian divide. Hezbollah has also used this new funding to obtain highly developed new armaments, including advanced technologies used by professional state militaries. While Hezbollah has been busy helping its Iranian masters prop up the brutal Assad regime in Syria, they have contracted out their violently anti-Israel agenda.

(1)

In 2016, Israeli authorities arrested a Palestinian cell organized and funded by Hezbollah that had planned to carry out suicide bombings. Iran also cemented its ties with the Palestinian terror group Hamas by providing them with missile technologies that enabled them to build their own rockets to target Israeli citizens. Iran helped Hamas build its terrorist tunnel infrastructure that was destroyed by Israel in 2014.

Since the nuclear deal, Iran terrorist plots have been uncovered in Kuwait, Bahrain, and Saudi Arabia. Hezbollah and Iran also remain active in Latin America where they operate criminal networks that yield even more money for Tehran to invest in terrorism. Back at home in Iran, the mullahs are busy dedicating more time and money to their ballistic missile program.

Since the announcement of the nuclear deal, Iran has conducted 14 ballistic missile tests. Earlier this month, Iran attempted to launch a cruise missile from one of its midget submarines, the same type of submarines the terrorist regime in North Korea is developing. Iran and North Korea are the only countries that deploy this class of submarine.

The failed test reminded the world of Iran and North Korea's long history of collaboration on this ballistic and even nuclear programs. Their dangerous relationship goes all the way back to the 1980s. Now the two rogue regimes are believed to be working on developing intercontinental ballistic missiles, ICBMs. Why is Iran moving ahead with a ballistic missile program? Because ballistic missiles are the best delivery system for nuclear weapons.

So while they wait 10 years till they can develop a bomb, Iran is ensuring they have the technology to deliver that payload. And there are some doubts about whether Iran is actually complying with the deal.

Members of the National Council of Resistance of Iran claimed last month that Iran is still working on weaponization, the final step on the path to nuclear weapons. It is clear this deal has allowed the mullahs to increase their support of terrorism and proliferation.

Leading up to the deal, the past administration assured us that the U.S. would continue to fight against Iran's maligned behavior. It is time now we get serious about that. We cannot allow Iran to continue threatening the United States and our allies unchecked. The question is: How do we do that? That is why we are having this hearing, and we have these three experts that will give us the answers to all of that.

And I will now yield to the gentleman from Massachusetts, Mr. Keating, for his opening statement.

Mr. KEATING. Thank you, Chairman Poe. And thank you for the witnesses that are here today to testify.

This hearing is very timely, coming less than a week after the reelection of Iranian President Rouhani, who was a key figure in reaching the nuclear agreement. It also comes at a time when President Trump is making his first trip abroad in the sphere threatened by Iran's malign acts. So it is fitting that we take up Iran in this subcommittee this afternoon, as this is a time when both countries are reassessing their security posture toward each other.

I supported, and continue to support, the Iran nuclear deal because it made us and our allies more secure and brought Iran more in line with international principles of nonproliferation. I also support aggressive, robust monitoring and enforcement of the deal so that we are certain that Iran never waivers in upholding their commitments under the agreement.

However, Iran's nuclear ambitions were not the only threat they posed to the region and to the United States' security interests. Iran has continued to conduct several ballistic missile tests in defiance of U.N. Security Council Resolution 2231, and to support terrorist organizations operating throughout the region, actively involved in the civil conflicts in Syria and in Yemen, and, as a result, is exacerbating the continued bloodshed in both countries, and further stalling resolutions to these conflicts.

Iran's human rights record is also appalling. Participation in civic life is severely restricted with the regular arrest of journalists and activists and repression of free speech, not to mention the ongoing imprisonment of American citizens. The United States' posture toward Iran must take into account all layers of Iran's aggressive stance toward the world.

However, that also includes taking into account the powerful role of Iranian public opinion. As we consider U.S. policies toward Iran and our response to Iranian threats to stability and security, we cannot do so without also considering Iran's domestic context, and recognizing that the President, President Rouhani, just received broad support from a diverse range of voters in Iran on Friday.

Here in Congress, and within the U.S. Government, we must be committed to curbing Iran's malign activities, and we must do so diligently. Iran's destabilizing action throughout the Middle East threatens the United States and must be met with clear condemnation for the sake of the countless human lives at stake and of the global rule of law. Yet we must take note of the complex reality that accounts for the domestic context in Iran today.

Therefore, I look forward to hearing from our witnesses and hear about how Congress can navigate these many security threats from Iran without running afoul of our international commitments, without backsliding on progress made so far and bringing Iran into compliance with international law and norms.

With the reelection of President Rouhani, I believe we must seize any possible opportunity to move forward in curbing Iran's support for terrorist organizations, undeterred ballistic missile testing, continued involvement in conflicts across the region, and its gross human rights violations. We should do so with the support of our allies, and our actions should be carried out swiftly, yet deliberately.

I thank the witnesses. I look forward to your testimony.

I yield back.

Mr. POE. I thank the gentleman for his comments.

The Chair will now have opening statements by members of the committee, 1-minute opening statements.

The Chair recognizes the gentleman from Florida, Mr. Mast.

Mr. MAST. Thank you for recognizing me. I appreciate it. And thank you for your testimonies.

I think it is important, on the heels of Memorial Day, that we really identify what it looks like for Iran to be the largest state sponsor of terrorists. It has become a phrase that has become so cliche in recent past. And what that really means, on the heels of Memorial Day, is it is Iranian hands that have made IEDs, the explosively formed projectiles that tore through our Up-Armored Humvees in Iraq. And it is Iranian hands that packed improvised explosive devices with nuts and screws and bolts and so many pieces of shrapnel that were placed in places like Afghanistan to put so many holes in our servicemembers that they could never be plugged before they bled out. That is what it looks like to be the largest state sponsor of terror. And I just think it is important that we keep that as a frame of reference, especially on the heels of Memorial Day, as we have this conversation.

I thank you for your time testifying today, and I look forward to hearing from you.

Mr. POE. I thank the gentleman from Florida.

The Chair will recognize the gentleman from Pennsylvania, Mr. Boyle.

Mr. BOYLE. Thank you to the chair and ranking member.

I would say that—and I happen to have been someone on the democratic side of the aisle who voted against the Iran deal. And I know there were good, principled arguments on both sides of that.

What I am most interested in, though, is not continuing to beat a dead horse of the political fight over this and moving beyond the politics of the deal, and whether or not it was a good idea, and accepting the reality, and moving forward. And, specifically, focusing on—my comments very much dovetail after the last ones we just heard—going after Iranian funding for Hamas, for Hezbollah, for their continued role in the Syrian civil war, for what they are doing in Yemen. I believe that should be our focus.

And rather than continuing to relitigate the past of the Iran deal, let's focus on that. Because, at the end of the day, it is cliche for a reason, they are the largest state sponsor of terrorism throughout the world. And that will continue unless we go after their funding.

Thank you. I yield back.

Mr. POE. The gentleman yields back his time.

Without objection, all of the witnesses' prepared statements will be made part of the record.

I ask that each witness keep their presentation to no more than 5 minutes. When the red light comes on in front of you, that means stop. And I will help you enforce that rule. I will introduce each witness and give them time for their opening statements.

Ilan Berman is the senior vice-president of the American Foreign Policy Council. He is an expert on regional security in the Middle East and has consulted for both the CIA and the Department of Defense.

Dr. Ray Takeyh is a senior fellow for Middle East studies at the Council of Foreign Relations. Prior to joining the CFR, he was a senior advisor on Iran at the State Department.

And Dr. Daniel Byman is a senior fellow in the Center for Middle East Policy at Brookings. His research focuses on counterterrorism and Middle East security.

Mr. Berman, we will start with you, and you have 5 minutes.

STATEMENT OF MR. ILAN BERMAN, SENIOR VICE PRESIDENT, AMERICAN FOREIGN POLICY COUNCIL

Mr. BERMAN. Thank you, Judge Poe. And thank you, Judge. And thank you, Ranking Member Keating. And I really appreciate the opportunity to be here today to discuss the 2015 nuclear deal between Iran and the P5+1 powers.

A good place to start is to recognize that more than a year after its implementation, the effects of the agreement have been profound, and they have been profoundly negative both for the stability of the Middle East and for American interests there. And much of this problem revolves around the fact that, while the agreement was only intended to be tactical in nature, to deal strictly with one aspect of the global threat that is posed by Iran, its effects for Iran have been both extensive and they have been strategic in nature.

Most notably—and I have a more detailed discourse in my written statement, which you have in front of you. But, most notably, I would point out that the JCPOA has had a material effect on reinvigorating the global ambitions of a regime that truly thinks globally, that thinks about itself as a regional hegemon and as a country with power projection capabilities far beyond its borders. And you can see this evident in several lines of effort that the Iranian regime is pursuing currently.

The first is a multispectrum military modernization that is both reinvigorated and is sustained in nature. And it encompasses things like the expansion of Iran's national defense budget to 5 percent of GDP; the acquisition of billions of dollars of new hardware from supplier states, like Russia and China; and substantially deeper investments in cyber warfare capabilities both for defense and for offense.

You can see Iran's focus on stepped-up regional activism, including greater assistance to the Assad regime in Syria, and also serving as a facilitator for a secondary state-directed foreign fighter flow that is bringing Afghans, Yemens, Shiites of non-Syrian origin to the Syrian battlefront. And you can see this in the solidification of Iranian influence over Iraqi politics through its extensive sponsorship of both Shiite militias and patronage of Shiite politicians in Iraq.

And, also, as all the members noted, you see a substantial surge in the amount of money, already extensive, that Iran has allocated toward the activities of organizations like Hezbollah in Lebanon and also in Syria and Hamas in the Palestinian territories.

The cumulative effect of this is that General Joseph Votel, the commander of U.S. Central Command, testified about approximately 1½ months ago, that these initiatives have made Iran "the most significant threat to the central region and to our national interests and to the interests of our partners and allies there." And I think that is a significant development. It is a significant escalation in the threat that is posed by Iran.

And this, I think, leads us to the question of: What can be done? I think that the Trump administration's Iran policy is still a work in progress. They are undergoing a comprehensive policy review that is going to touch on all aspects of Iran policy, including the nuclear deal, and other issues. But, as they do, I think they would be very well-advised to focus on four priorities.

The first is to reestablish economic leverage over Iran. The JCPOA has put in motion a fundamental unraveling of the global sanctions regime against Iran for a host of reasons. And Washington needs to restore the economic leverage that it once had against Iran, and it can do so through measures like the additional blacklisting of entities engaged in illicit behavior, and also a comprehensive blacklisting on the Iranian Revolutionary Guard Corps, which controls a third or more of Iran's national economy.

The second priority should be to ensure compliance with the terms of the nuclear deal. Because as much as termination of the JCPOA was a campaign issue last year, it is abundantly clear that the contours of the agreement will remain in force, at least for the near future. And that means that we have to focus on ensuring compliance, in material terms, the hiring of additional inspectors, gaining access to facilities that are currently obscured, and, most of all, constructing a menu that talks about what constitutes a material breach of the agreement so that all the members of the P5+1 can be on the same page about whether Iran is in violation of its obligations.

Very briefly, the other two priorities that the administration should focus on would be mechanisms by which it can constrain Iranian expansionism, to include the construction of a regional security architecture very much along the lines of what the Trump administration has begun discussing in its current trip to the Middle East.

And, lastly, the reconstruction of American credibility, vis-a-vis, the Iranian people. Historically, the United States has served as a champion for ordinary Iranians in their struggle against the clerical state. This is a moral high ground that the U.S. has retreated from over the last 8 years in the service of a tactical arrangement with the Iranian regime. And this is ground that we need to make up. And we can make this up in a number of different ways, from different statements, to more robust broadcasting, to other demonstrations of the fact that this administration is not prepared to accept the current political status quo in Tehran.

And the time to do so, in my opinion, is now. The U.S. Government needs to move robustly to implement a new approach that begins to roll back Iranian influence and activities in the region, activities that have been emboldened, in no small measure, by the agreement that was signed in July 2015.

Thank you.

[The prepared statement of Mr. Berman follows:]

American Foreign Policy Council

Congressional Testimony

Nuclear Deal Fallout: The Global Threat of Iran

Ilan Berman
AFPC Senior Vice President

Statement before the House Foreign Affairs Committee
Subcommittee on Terrorism, Nonproliferation, and Trade

May 24, 2017

American Foreign Policy Council

Chairman Poe, Ranking Member Keating, distinguished members of the Subcommittee:

It is a privilege to appear before you today to discuss the strategic effects of the 2015 nuclear deal between Iran and the P5+1 powers, formally known as the Joint Comprehensive Plan of Action (JCPOA). More than a year after its implementation, the effects of that agreement have been profound—and profoundly negative for the stability of the Middle East, as well as for American interests there.

FRUITS OF THE NUCLEAR DEAL

From the start, the accord concluded between Iran and the P5+1 was intended to be tactical in nature, focusing on just one aspect of the Iranian regime's rogue behavior: its persistent nuclear ambitions. However, the benefits that have been conferred to Iran as a result have been both extensive and strategic in nature.

Most directly, as a core condition of the JCPOA, the United States and its partners in the P5+1 agreed to release to Iran some $100 billion or more in previously escrowed oil revenue. For Iran, this represents an enormous windfall, amounting to roughly a quarter of its annual GDP, which totaled $415 billion in 2014.[1] By way of comparison, that sum nearly rivals the entirety of the European Recovery Program (colloquially known as the Marshall Plan) launched by the Truman administration in 1948 in the aftermath of World War II—an initiative that disbursed more than $13 billion (roughly $130 billion in today's dollars) to seventeen countries in Europe over the span of four years. As of "Implementation Day" (January 16, 2016), the Islamic Republic has complete, unencumbered access to these funds.

This direct benefit, moreover, has been amplified by a range of other measures, such as the reintegration of Iran into global markets via mechanisms like the electronic payment system run by the Society for Worldwide Interbank Financial Telecommunications (SWIFT),[2] as well as by the easing of multilateral restrictions on international involvement in Iran's economic sector. The cumulative impact has been profound; Iran's economy, which was teetering on the brink of collapse in the Fall of 2013, is now on a path of sustained growth, according to the estimates of international financial institutions such as the International Monetary Fund and World Bank.[3]

Notably, however, this newfound prosperity has not trickled down to the average Iranian. A January 2017 survey of Iranian public opinion conducted by the Center for International Security Studies at the University of Maryland found a broad consensus among respondents that, a year on, "there have been no improvements in people's living conditions as a result of the nuclear deal."[4] This, in turn, has

---

[1] "Iran GDP: 1965-2017," *Trading Economics*, n.d., http://www.tradingeconomics.com/iran/gdp.

[2] "Iranian Banks Reconnected to SWIFT Network after Four-Year Hiatus," Reuters, February 17, 2016, http://www.reuters.com/article/us-iran-banks-swift-idUSKCN0VQ1FD.

[3] See, for example, International Monetary Fund, "Iran: Concluding Statement of an IMF Staff Visit," October 3, 2016, http://www.imf.org/en/News/Articles/2016/10/03/MS100316-Iran-Concluding-Statement-of-an-IMF-Staff-Visit.

[4] Nancy Gallagher, Ebrahim Mohseni and Clay Ramsay, "Iranian Attitudes on Iranian-U.S. Relations in the Trump Era," Center for International & Security Studies at Maryland CISSM Report, January 2017. http://www.cissm.umd.edu/publications/iranian-attitudes-iranian-us-relations-trump-era.

American Foreign Policy Council

led to declining enthusiasm for the nuclear deal within Iranian society, and helped make the agreement a significant political issue in the country's most recent presidential contest, which concluded in recent days.[5]

Nor has the agreement yielded a fundamental change in Iran's political outlook. Contrary to the fervent wishes of the Obama administration, the JCPOA did not foster a kinder, gentler polity within the Islamic Republic. While the Obama White House lobbied heavily in favor of the agreement based on the argument that it would help empower moderate forces within Iran,[6] nothing of the sort has happened. Instead, last summer's elections for Iran's parliament, or *majles*, saw a resounding reaffirmation of the conservative *status quo* in Iranian politics.[7] So the situation has remained, notwithstanding the electoral victory of incumbent President Hassan Rouhani in last week's presidential run-off.

What the JCPOA has succeeded in doing, however, is reinvigorating the global ambitions of the Iranian regime. After laboring for years under international sanctions and with limited means to make its foreign policy vision a reality, the Islamic Republic is now in the throes of a landmark expansion of both its regional activities and its strategic capabilities.

- Long moribund as a result of international sanctions, the Iranian regime's military modernization efforts have now shifted into high gear. In June of 2015, ahead of the formal conclusion of the JCPOA, Iranian Supreme Leader Ali Khamenei formally unveiled his government's Sixth Development Plan, which outlines its intent to expand the national defense budget (then at $14 billion) by nearly a third, to five percent of total GDP[8]—a surge predicated entirely on Iran's ability to access additional resources as a result of the nuclear deal. Since then, Tehran has concluded tens of billions of dollars in new accords for military hardware and materiel with both Russia and China.[9] Over time, this drive can be expected to significantly expand the Iranian regime's strategic capabilities, as well as the potential threat that it can pose to U.S. and allied forces in the Middle Eastern theater.
- While not yet a first-tier cyber power like Russia and China, Iran is nonetheless fast emerging as a significant threat actor in cyberspace. Over the past several years, the Iranian regime has made the strengthening of its cyber capabilities a major priority. The results have been visible in a spate of high-profile cyber attacks against both U.S. and international targets carried out by the regime and affiliated actors over the past half-decade. And while such instances have declined since the signing of the JCPOA (reflecting Iran's satisfaction with the terms of the agreement), the Iranian regime

[5] See Ilan Berman, "The JCPOA Helps Iran's Elites and Hurts Rouhani," *Foreign Affairs*, March 29, 2017, https://www.foreignaffairs.com/articles/iran/2017-03-29/jcpoa-helps-irans-elites-and-hurts-rouhani?cid=int-lea&pgtype=hpg.
[6] "Transcript: President Obama's Full NPR Interview On Iran Nuclear Deal," *NPR*, April 7, 2015, http://www.npr.org/2015/04/07/397933577/transcript-president-obamas-full-npr-interview-on-iran-nuclear-deal.
[7] Shashank Bengali and Ramin Mostaghim, "Did Iran's Reformists Celebrate too Soon? Hard-liners Rebound After Election," *Los Angeles Times*, June 1, 2016, http://www.latimes.com/world/la-fg-iran-hardliners-20160601-snap-story.html.
[8] Abbas Qaidaari, "More Planes, More Missiles, More Warships: Iran Increases its military budget by a third," *Al-Monitor*, July 13, 2015, http://www.al-monitor.com/pulse/originals/2015/07/khamenei-orders-increase-military.html.
[9] See, for example, Adam Kredo, "Report: Iran Ramping Up Military Purchases from Russia, China," *Washington Free Beacon*, October 13, 2015, http://freebeacon.com/national-security/report-iran-ramping-up-military-purchases-from-russia-china/.

American Foreign Policy Council

is nonetheless making major investments in its cyber capabilities. Since 2013, Iran is estimated to have increased its overall cybersecurity spending twelve-fold,[10] with the IRGC now boasting an annual cyber budget of nearly $20 million.[11] This surge accurately reflects the Islamic Republic's interest in the exploitation of cyberspace for both defensive and offensive purposes—a maturing capability that could be used against the United States and allied nations in the event of a conflict.

- Since the start of the Syrian civil war in 2011, Iran has emerged as a key player in that conflict, providing extensive arms, training and materiel to the regime of Syrian dictator Bashar al-Assad. More recently, the Islamic Republic has become a major conduit for foreign fighters as well. Working together with its Lebanese proxy, Hezbollah, the Iranian regime has played a key role in organizing pro-Assad militias among the country's Alawite and Shi'a communities, as well as coordinating pro-regime foreign fighters from Iraq, Yemen, Lebanon and Afghanistan.[12] As of January 2017, this secondary, state-directed foreign fighter stream was estimated to number as many as 20,000 "volunteers."[13]

- Iran's activism elsewhere in the region has surged as well. In Yemen, the Islamic Republic has emerged as a significant source of support for the country's Houthi rebels, providing vital weaponry as well as sustained logistical, political, and financial support to the rebellion.[14] This assistance was crucial to the Fall 2014 Houthi takeover of portions of the Yemeni capital, Sana'a, and their consolidation of power (and periodic targeting of Western interests) since. In Iraq as well, Iran's historic asymmetric strategy—pursued since 2003 and intended "to limit American power-projection capability in the Middle East, ensure the Iraqi government does not pose a threat to Iran, and build a reliable platform for projecting influence further abroad"[15]—has expanded significantly. In response to the rise of the Islamic State terrorist group (ISIS), the Islamic Republic has commenced a major mobilization, providing both arms and advisors to Kurdish peshmerga guerrillas battling ISIS in northern Iraq,[16] and sending detachments of its Revolutionary Guards to fight the group on Iraqi soil.[17] It has also organized and deployed some 40 Iraqi Shi'a militias against ISIS.[18] Pursuant to a

[10] "Iran Is Building a Non-nuclear Threat Faster than Experts Would have Imagined," *Business Insider*, March 27, 2013, http://www.businessinsider.com/irans-cyber-army-2015-3.

[11] Small Media, "Iranian Internet Infrastructure and Policy Report: The Rouhani Review (2013-15)," February 2015, https://smallmedia.org.uk/sites/default/files/u8/IIIP_Feb15.pdf.

[12] See, for example, Farnaz Fassihi, "Iran Recruiting Afghan Refugees to Fight for Regime in Syria," *Wall Street Journal*, May 15, 2014, online.wsj.com/news/articles/SB10001424052702304908304579564161508613846?mg=reno64-ws-j&url=http%3A%2F%2Fonline.wsj.com%2Farticle%2FSB10001424052702304908304579564161508613846.html.

[13] See, for example, Ahmad Majidyar, "Iran Recruits and Trains Large Numbers of Afghan and Pakistani Shiites," Middle East Institute, January 18, 2017, http://www.mei.edu/content/article/io/iran-s-recruitment-afghan-pakistani-shiites-further-destabilizes-south-asia.

[14] Robert F. Worth, and C. J. Chivers, "Seized Arms Off Yemen Raise Alarm Over Iran," *New York Times*, March 2, 2013, http://www.nytimes.com/2013/03/03/world/middleeast/seized-arms-off-yemen-raise-alarm-over-iran.html; Hakim Almasmari, "Houthi Official Denies Receiving Arms from Iran," *The National*, March 16, 2012, http://www.thenational.ae/news/world/middle-east/houthi-official-denies-receiving-arms-from-iran.

[15] Joseph Felter and Brian Fishman, "Iranian Strategy in Iraq: Politics and 'Other Means,'" Combatting Center at West Point Occasional Paper, October 13, 2008, http://reap2-ws1.stanford.edu/publications/iranian_strategy_in_iraq_politics_and_other_means/.

[16] Arash Karami, "Iran Interior Minister Says Advisers Sent to Iraqi Kurdistan," *Al-Monitor*, August 26, 2014, http://www.al-monitor.com/pulse/originals/2014/08/iran-sends-advisers-kurdistan-region-iraq.html#ixzz3CTppCln9.

[17] Babak Dehghanpisheh, "Iran's Elite Guards Fighting in Iraq to Push Back Islamic State," Reuters, August 3, 2014,

American Foreign Policy Council

December 2016 law passed by the Iraqi government, these militias are now officially considered a part of Iraq's armed forces, giving the Iranian regime significant influence over Iraq's future political direction. All told, Iran can now be said to control four separate Arab capitals: Beirut, Lebanon; Damascus, Syria; Sana'a, Yemen; and Baghdad, Iraq.

- Iran's regime has historically served as the world's leading state sponsor of terrorism, providing economic support to a range of radical causes. At the time of the signing of the JCPOA in the summer of 2015, the Congressional Research Service estimated that the Islamic Republic was spending between $3.5 billion to $16 billion annually on terrorism and insurgency worldwide, including bankrolling the entire operating budget of the Palestinian Islamic Jihad terrorist organization, providing tens of millions of dollars to the Hamas terrorist group, and transferring between $100 and $200 million annually to Lebanon's Hezbollah militia.[19] The concrete economic benefits of the JCPOA have allowed Iran to expand this sponsorship significantly. According to Middle Eastern sources, Iran has ramped up its support to Hamas in recent weeks, including the provision of as much as $27 million to the Palestinian movement.[20] Iranian aid to Hezbollah is also believed to have ballooned to as much as $1 billion annually in recent times.[21]

The cumulative impact of these developments is that Iran now represents "the most significant threat to the Central Region and to our national interests and the interests of our partners and allies," in the judgment of Gen. Joseph Votel, the commander of U.S. Central Command.[22]

COPING WITH AN EMBOLDENED IRAN

How can the United States best counter the expanding threat posed by the Islamic Republic? The Trump administration is currently in the midst of a comprehensive review of U.S. policy toward Iran, and that process can be expected to yield significant changes to both the way the new White House approaches both the 2015 nuclear deal and Iran's broader activities in the Middle East. As it formulates its approach, the Administration should focus on four distinct priorities:

---

http://www.reuters.com/article/2014/08/03/us-iraq-security-iran-insight-idUSKBN0G30GE20140803.

[18] Mustafa Saadoun, "PMU Seeks to Secure Iraq-Syria Border," *Al-Monitor*, December 20, 2016, http://www.al-monitor.com/pulse/originals/2016/12/iraq-syria-pmu-iran-isis.html.

[19] Carla Humud, Christopher Blanchard, Jeremy Sharp and Jim Zanotti, "Iranian Assistance to Groups in Yemen, Iraq, Syria, and the Palestinian Territories," Congressional Research Service *Memorandum*, July 31, 2015, http://www.kirk.senate.gov/images/PDF/Iran%20Financial%20Support%20to%20Terrorists%20and%20Militants.pdf.

[20] See, for example, "Iran Extends Its Hand to Alkassam Brigades," *Al Modon*, May 4, 2017, http://www.almodon.com/arabworld/2017/5/4/%D9%85%D8%B5%D8%A7%D8%AF%D8%B1-%D8%A7%D9%84%D9%82%D8%B3%D8%A7%D9%85-%D8%AA%D9%84%D9%82%D8%AA-%D9%A2%D9%A7-%D9%85%D9%84%D9%8A%D9%88%D9%86-%D8%AF%D9%88%D9%84%D8%A7%D8%B1-%D9%85%D9%86-%D8%A5%D9%8A%D8%B1%D8%A7%D9%86.

[21] See, for example, Walter Wolowedsk, "The Decline of the Secret Superpower in the Middle East," *Die Welt* (Berlin), April 28, 2017, https://www.welt.de/politik/ausland/article163910675/Der-Niedergang-der-geheimen-Grossmacht-im-Nahen-Osten.html.

[22] General Joseph L. Votel, Statement for the Record Before the House Armed Services Committee, March 15, 2017, http://docs.house.gov/meetings/AS/AS00/20170329/105692/HHRG-115-AS00-Wstate-VotelJ-20170329.pdf.

American Foreign Policy Council

Reestablishing Economic Leverage

Perhaps the most pernicious effect of the JCPOA has been to set in motion a fundamental unraveling of the global sanctions regime against Iran. The Obama administration's efforts in support of the agreement—including attempts to encourage greater international commerce with Iran and the assumption of a direct investment role in Iran's nuclear program[23]—helped to compromise the integrity of the sanctions architecture that had been painstakingly erected against the Islamic Republic over the preceding decade-and-a-half. A key future priority of the U.S. government, therefore, must be to restore the economic leverage that Washington once wielded over Tehran.

The Trump administration has far more clout to do so than is commonly understood. Since the signing of the JCPOA (and despite the Obama administration's best efforts to encourage trade normalization with Iran), banks and other financial institutions have proven generally timid in reengaging the Islamic Republic, fearful of the potential consequences of doing so.[24] That caution was reinforced by Mr. Trump's election in November, and by the widespread view that his administration is prepared to apply greater economic pressure than its predecessor against both Tehran and its trading partners. However, such hesitance is not a permanent condition, and over time companies and banks can be expected to grow bolder in their pursuit of new business opportunities with the Iranian regime. As a result, the new administration needs to move resolutely to enact measures (such as the blacklisting of Iranian individuals and entities suspected of illicit activity, and the levying of onerous fines on those doing business with them) which send a clear signal that it will not condone a return to "business as usual" with the Islamic Republic. As of last week, it appears to have begun this process.[25]

Perhaps the most promising step that can be taken in this regard is a comprehensive blacklisting of Iran's clerical army, the Islamic Revolutionary Guard Corps (*Sepāh-e Pāsdārān-e Enqelāb-e Eslāmi, IRGC*). That idea, floated in the early days of the Trump administration, deserves a serious second look by both the White House and Congress. This is because the IRGC is an economic powerhouse, in control of a sprawling empire of companies and corporate entities within the Islamic Republic. All told, the IRGC is believed to command as much as one-third of the country's total economy.[26] As a result, a comprehensive designation would have a profound impact, rendering large swathes of the Iranian economy (such as its construction and telecom sectors) radioactive as a matter of trade policy, and thereby helping prevent a further normalization of international trade with Iran. Of equal significance,

---

[23] See, for example, Michele Kelemen, "John Kerry's Awkward Push For Investment In Iran," *NPR*, May 25, 2016, http://www.npr.org/sections/parallels/2016/05/25/479462791/john-kerrys-awkward-push-for-investment-in-iran; See also Jay Solomon, "U.S. To Buy Material Used In Iran Nuclear Program," *Wall Street Journal*, April 22, 2016, https://www.wsj.com/articles/u-s-to-buy-material-used-in-iran-nuclear-program-1461319381.

[24] Gillian Tett, "Banks Cannot Invest in Iran Without US Guarantees," *Financial Times*, August 26, 2016, https://www.ft.com/content/f7dfa16c-69f3-11e6-ae5b-a7cc5dd5a28c.

[25] U.S. Department of the Treasury, "Treasury Sanctions Iranian Defense Officials and a China-based Network for Supporting Iran's Ballistic Missile Program," May 17, 2017, https://www.treasury.gov/press-center/press-releases/Pages/sm0088.aspx.

[26] See, for example, Mark Gregory, "Expanding Business Empire of Iran's Revolutionary Guards," *BBC*, July 26, 2010, http://www.bbc.com/news/world-middle-east-10743580.

American Foreign Policy Council

a ban would send a major warning to international firms and foreign nations now beginning to dip their toes back into the Iranian market that, if they continue to do so, they are in danger of running afoul of U.S. counterterrorism laws, with potentially disastrous monetary and political consequences.

Ensuring Compliance

While the abrogation of the JCPOA emerged as a major campaign issue during the 2016 election, it is increasingly clear that the Trump administration will continue to abide by the terms of the agreement, at least for the foreseeable future. There are practical reasons for this; the multilateral nature of the JCPOA means that a U.S. withdrawal from its terms would not automatically trigger its collapse, and a meaningful rollback of the deal may not be possible without provoking major trade disputes with counties such as China and France—something which the Trump administration, despite its commitment to a more coercive Iran policy, is nonetheless eager to avoid. As a result, the new Administration is likely to remain within the confines of the JCPOA in the near term, even while it attempts to significantly adapt and strengthen its provisions and penalties.

There is a great deal that must be done in this regard. During its time in office, the Obama administration proved loathe to hold the Iranian regime accountable for substantive breaches of the accord itself, or for related activities (such as ballistic missile testing) that violated its spirit. The Trump administration must take a more active role in tracking Iran's compliance with the terms of the JCPOA, including by ensuring the hiring and deployment of additional inspectors to Iran's nuclear facilities, and by demanding access from Iran to additional nuclear facilities not currently being monitored under the terms of the deal. The White House should also consider constructing an explicit menu of what constitutes a "material breach" of the JCPOA (and which enumerates the concrete penalties associated with such violations) as a way of eliminating ambiguities and political disputes that prompted the Obama administration to turn a blind eye to Iranian infractions in the past.

Constraining Iranian Expansionism

More than a year after "implementation," there is no shortage of evidence that the benefits of the JCPOA have enabled a significant strategic expansion on the part of the Iranian regime, with concrete negative effects for regional security. For Washington, reinforcing stability in the Middle East will hinge on constraining Iran's advances, and implementing policies that can serve to deter or counterbalance future Iranian adventurism.

One such initiative is the creation of a regional security architecture encompassing countries in the Islamic Republic's immediate periphery. Such a regional partnership would help to expand America's relationship with the Gulf States, and transform the GCC into an operational military alliance capable of deterring the Iranian regime. Notably, movement in this direction appears to already be underway; the President's visit to the Middle East has entailed significant efforts to erect an "Arab NATO" capable of serving, in part, as a counterweight against Iran.[27]

---

[27] Josh Rogin, "Trump to Unveil Plans for an 'Arab NATO' in Saudi Arabia," *Washington Post*, May 17, 2017, https://www.washingtonpost.com/news/josh-rogin/wp/2017/05/17/trump-to-unveil-plans-for-an-arab-nato-in-saudi-arabia/?utm_term=.90afe1cea21a.

American Foreign Policy Council

A blacklisting of the IRGC could provide benefits in this arena as well. U.S. forces have labored for years under restrictive "rules of engagement" in the Iraqi theater due to worries that battlefield contact with Iranian paramilitary elements could result in an uncontrolled escalation of hostilities between Washington and Tehran. This has hampered the effectiveness of U.S. counterinsurgency and stability operations, and continues to exert a profound effect on the freedom of action that field commanders believe they possess today. In turn, U.S. military officials have been outspoken about the destabilizing role being played by Iran in the region and about the need to push back forcefully against it.[28] A blacklisting of the IRGC would begin that process by providing U.S. commanders with greater authority to counter Iranian destabilizing behavior on the ground throughout their area of responsibility.

Rebuilding American Credibility

Historically, and in spite of its limited ability to affect internal change, the United States has been viewed by ordinary Iranians as a champion of their struggle against the repressive, theocratic Iranian state. During its time in office, however, the Obama administration progressively ceded this moral high ground. In its pursuit of accommodation with the Iranian regime, the previous administration focused less and less upon the plight and potential of the Iranian people, and more and more on ingratiating itself with the repressive government that ruled over them, culminating in the signing of the JCPOA in 2015.

An important priority for the Trump administration, therefore, must be to reestablish the credibility of the United States in the minds of the Iranian people. This requires that the White House articulate, and then demonstrate, that it is not content with the current political *status quo* within the Islamic Republic. High-profile political steps, such as a comprehensive blacklisting of the IRGC, could send a potent message to Iranian and international audiences alike that the United States is no longer prepared to pursue "business as usual" with Iran's ayatollahs. So could official messaging that focuses more intently on highlighting endemic corruption within the Iranian regime, the country's repressive domestic practices, the Iranian regime's failure to provide broad-based prosperity (despite the material benefits of the JCPOA), and the plight of individual political prisoners within the Islamic Republic. The goal of such messaging should be strategic: to diminish the credibility and authority of Iran's clerical regime, and to increase that of the United States.

---

[28] See, for example, Jeff Daniels, "General Calls Iran 'Destabilizing' Force, Suggests US 'Disrupt' Regime by Military Means," *CNBC*, March 29, 2017, http://www.cnbc.com/2017/03/29/general-calls-iran-destabilizing-force-suggests-us-disrupt-regime-by-military-means.html.

American Foreign Policy Council

Ilan Berman
Senior Vice President, AFPC

Ilan Berman is Senior Vice President of the American Foreign Policy Council in Washington, DC. An expert on regional security in the Middle East, Central Asia, and the Russian Federation, he has consulted for both the U.S. Central Intelligence Agency and the U.S. Department of Defense, and provided assistance on foreign policy and national security issues to a range of governmental agencies and congressional offices. He has been called one of America's "leading experts on the Middle East and Iran" by CNN.

Mr. Berman is a member of the Associated Faculty at Missouri State University's Department of Defense and Strategic Studies. A frequent writer and commentator, he has written for the *Wall Street Journal*, *Foreign Affairs*, the *New York Times*, *Foreign Policy*, the *Washington Post* and *USA Today*, among many other publications.

Mr. Berman is the editor of three books - *Dismantling Tyranny: Transitioning Beyond Totalitarian Regimes* (Rowman & Littlefield, 2005), co-edited with J. Michael Waller *Taking on Tehran: Strategies for Confronting the Islamic Republic* (Rowman & Littlefield, 2007), and *Iran's Strategic Penetration of Latin America* (Lexington Books, 2015), co-edited with Joseph Humire - and the author of four others: *Tehran Rising: Iran's Challenge to the United States* (Rowman & Littlefield, 2005), *Winning the Long War: Retaking the Offensive Against Radical Islam* (Rowman & Littlefield, 2009), *Implosion: The End of Russia and What It Means for America* (Regnery Publishing, 2013), and most recently, *Iran's Deadly Ambition: The Islamic Republic's Quest for Global Power* (Encounter Books, 2015).

About AFPC

For more than three decades, the American Foreign Policy Council (AFPC) has played an important role in the U.S. foreign policy debate. Founded in 1982, AFPC is a non-profit organization dedicated to bringing information to those who make or influence the foreign policy of the United States. AFPC is widely recognized as a source of timely, insightful analysis on issues of foreign policy, and works closely with members of Congress, the Executive Branch and the policymaking community. It is staffed by noted specialists in foreign and defense policy, and serves as a valuable resource to officials in the highest levels of government.

Mr. POE. Thank you, Mr. Berman.
Dr. Takeyh.

STATEMENT OF RAY TAKEYH, PH.D., HASIB J. SABBAGH SENIOR FELLOW FOR MIDDLE EAST STUDIES, COUNCIL ON FOREIGN RELATIONS

Mr. TAKEYH. Thank you.

I know from previous representations in front of Judge Poe, 5 minutes means 5 minutes. So I will stay diligently within the timeframe that I am sure you will insist upon.

Terrorism, the use of political violence, is an enduring aspect of the Islamic Republic. The regime's victims, as was mentioned, span the region. But the most vulnerable targets of that state-sponsored violence have always been the Iranian people themselves.

The key actors defining Iran's regional policies are not its diplomats but its Revolutionary Guard Corp, particularly the famed Quds Brigade. For the commander of the Quds Brigade, General Soleimani, the struggle to evict America from the region began in Iraq, has now moved to Syria. For the hardliners, the Sunni states' attempt to dislodge Bashar Assad is really a means of weakening Iran. Thus, the survival or the success of the Assad regime at this point is one of the central elements of the Iranian foreign policy. The question then becomes what impact the nuclear deal have on Iran and its regional surge. The proponents of the agreement at one point insisted that whatever windfall there was would be fun- neled for domestic purposes and Iran's depleted economy. By their telling, Iran had prioritized its malign activities even during the times of economic stress. Two years later, we see some of the aspects of those claims cannot be substantiated.

Iran's defense budget has gone up by about 50 percent. It used to be about 2.7 percent of the GDP. Between now and year 2020, it is likely to be 5 percent of the GDP. So it has about doubled.

Iran's model for operating in the Middle East today is drawn from its experiences in Lebanon in the early 1980s. It was at that time that Iran amalgamated various Shia parties into the lethal Hezbollah. In essence, Iran created a militia outside the control of the weak Lebanese state. In the meantime, Iran sought to manipulate the politics of Lebanon to its advantage by making sure that the central government remains weak.

A decentralized state not in full command of coercive power is a model that Iran has used first in Lebanon and now in Iraq and, of course, in Syria.

Since the U.S. invasion of Iraq in 2003, Iran has sought to take advantage of the disorder there and extend its influence. The Islamic Republic has trained Shia militias, as was mentioned, that are responsive to its orders and has sought to sharpen the sectarian divides in Iraq as a means of dividing that nation against itself. The rise of the Islamic State has actually provided Iran an opportunity for further inroads in Iraq. Under the auspices of fighting the Islamic State, Iran has further projected its power in that nation. So long as Iraq's trouble continues, Iran can be counted on to further exacerbate them.

Since the beginning of the Syrian civil war, Iranian officials maintained that the Assad regime will survive. This assessment stood in contrast to those Western powers who assure themselves that the forward march of history would envelop the Syrian dictator. The Iranian model of operation in Syria, again, is very much similar to that of Iraq and, previous to that, Lebanon.

Once more, Iran deployed to develop militias outside the control of the state, deployed a large number of Revolutionary Guards and Hezbollah proxies, and, essentially, took command of the ground forces. Without Iranian assistance and guidance, Syrians may have been spared some of the carnage that has wrecked their country. Supreme Leader Ali Khamenei today stands as the most success- ful Persian imperialist in the history of Iran. In the 1970s, at the height of his power, the Shah did not enjoy commanding influence in Iraq, Lebanon's confessional politics eluded him, and the Assad regime was not a mere subsidiary of Iran, and the Persian Gulf States resisted his pretensions.

Today, Iran has essential control of much of the Iraqi state. It is the most important external actor in Syria, and Hezbollah provides it with not just means of manipulating Lebanese politics, but also shock troops that can be deployed in various war fronts.

It is important to appreciate that, actually, Israel remains the principal victim of Iranian terrorism. Iran's hostility toward Israel is one of the most enduring and perplexing aspects of its history. Iran's animosity toward Israel can be traced back to the founding of its revolution. In the eyes of the founder of the revolution, the creation of Israel was the most unforgettable sin. In a perverse way, Iran's opposition to Israel exceeds even its opposition to the United States, because it objects to various American acts, not to its existence as it does with Israel.

A regime as dangerous to U.S. interests as Islamic Republic requires, as was mentioned, a comprehensive strategy to counter it. This means exploiting all of Iran's vulnerabilities, increasing the cost of its foreign adventures, weakening its economy, supporting its domestic discontents. Pursuing this strategy will take time, but, eventually, it will put the United States in a position to impose terms on Iran. And we should, as was mentioned, put human rights at the top of the agenda, not look the other way as Iran's leaders oppress their people.

And my time has ran out exactly at 5 minutes.

[The prepared statement of Mr. Takeyh follows:]

The Nuclear Dal Fallout: The Global Threat of Iran

Prepared Statement by

Ray Takeyh

Hasib J Sabbagh Senior Fellow for Middle East Studies, Council on Foreign Relations

Before the Subcommittee on Terrorism, Nonproliferation, and Trade
The Committee on Foreign Affairs

For much of the past three decades, the Islamic Republic's inflammatory rhetoric and aggressive posture concealed a measure of strategic loneliness. Iran is, after all, a Persian nation surrounded by Arab states who were suspicious of it revolution and its proclaimed objectives. The Gulf nations arrayed themselves behind the American shield, Iraq sustained its animosity toward Iran long after the end of its long war, and the incumbent Sunni republics maintained a steady belligerence. Iran nurtured its lethal Hezbollah protégé and aided Palestinian rejectionist groups, but appeared hemmed in by the wall of Arab hostility. All this changed when Iraq was reclaimed by the Shias and the Arab Spring shook the foundations of the Sunni order.

The key actors defining Iran's regional policy are not its diplomats mingling with their Western counterparts, but the Revolutionary Guards, particularly the famed Quds Brigade. For the commander of the Quds Brigade, General Qassim Soleimani, the struggle to evict America from the region began in Iraq and has now moved on to Syria. For the hardliners, the Sunni states attempting to dislodge Bashir Assad is really a means of weakening Iran. The survival and success of the Assad dynasty is now a central element of Iran's foreign policy.

The question then becomes what impact the nuclear did have on Iran and its regional surge? The proponents of the agreement insisted that Iran would funnel much of this newfound wealth into its depleted economy. By their telling, even during economic times, Iran prioritized funding for its malign activities and thus did not need to steer new money in their direction. Two years later, we see the hollowness of those claims. Iran's defense budget has more than doubled since the advent of the nuclear deal and its activities in both Iran and Syria have intensified.

The proponents of the view that Iran would not become a more aggressive regional power as a result of the deal ignored how the Middle East has evolved since the Arab awakenings. The post-colonial Arab state system that featured the dominant nations of Egypt and Iraq is no more. Egypt is too preoccupied with its internal squabbles to offer regional leadership while Iraq is a fragmented nation ruled by a Shia government ostracized from Sunni Arab councils. Iran has embarked on a dramatic new mission and is seeking to project its power into corners of the Middle East in ways that were never possible before. This is not the traditional Iranian foreign policy with its sponsorship of terrorism and support for rejectionist groups targeting Israel; imperialism beckons the mullahs but it is also economically burdensome. Without an arms control agreement and the financial rewards it offered—such as sanctions relief, the release of entrapped funds abroad, and new investments—Iran would find it difficult to subsidize its imperial surge.

Iran's model of operating in the Middle East today is drawn from its experience in Lebanon in the 1980s. It was at that time that Iran amalgamated various Shia parties into the lethal Hezbollah. In essence, Iran created a militia that was outside the control of the weak Lebanese state. In the meantime, Iran sought to manipulate the politics of Lebanon to its advantage by making sure that a strong central government did not emerge in Beirut. A de-centralized state that in full command of its coercive power is a model that Iran has used first in Lebanon and now in Iraq and Syria.

Since the U.S. invasion of Iraq in 2003, Iran has sought to take advantage of the disorder there to extend its influence. The Islamic Republic has trained Shia militias responsive to its orders and has sought to sharpen the sectarian divides in Iraq as a means of dividing that nation against itself. The rise of the Islamic State (ISIS) provided Iran with an opportunity for further inroads in Iraq. Under the auspices of fighting the Islamic State, Iran has further projected its power in that hapless nation. So long as Iraq's troubles continue, Iran can be counted on to further exacerbate them. The additional funds that the JCPOA has provided Iran are indispensable for its operations there.

Since the onset of the Syrian civil war, Iranian officials maintained that Assad would survive. This assessments stood in stark contrast to that of the Western powers who assured themselves that the forward march of history would envelop the Syrian despot. The Iranian model of operation in Syria was eerily similar to the one they used in Iraq and before than in Lebanon. Once more, Iran developed militias outside state control, deploy an increasing large number of its Revolutionary Guards and Hezbollah proxies and essentially took command of the ground operations. Assad's war crimes are Khamenei's war crimes as well. Without Iranian assistance and guidance, Syria may have been spared the carnage that has wrecked that country.

Supreme Leader Ali Khamenei stands as one of the most successful Persian imperialists in the history of modern Iran. In the 1970s, at the height of his power, the shah did not enjoy the commanding influence in Iraq, Lebanon's factional politics continued to elude him, the Assad dynasty was no mere subsidiary of Iran, and the Persian Gulf emirates resisted his pretensions. Today, Khamenei has essential control of much of the Iraqi state, he is the most important external actor in Syria, and Hezbollah provides him with not just a means of manipulating Lebanon's politics, but also shock troops who can be deployed on various war fronts. In the Gulf, the previous American indifference offered Iran many temptations.

Iran, Israel and the Instruments of Terrorism

It is important to appreciate that Israel remains the principal victim of Iranian terrorism. Iran's hostility toward Israel is one of the most enduring and perplexing aspects of the Middle East conflict. Since the inception of the Islamic Republic, Iran's clerical politicians have persistently denounced Israel and questioned its legitimacy, if not the right to exist. This is curious, as Iran has never fought a war with Israel and has no territorial disputes with the Jewish state. Indeed, Israel and Iran under the shah had established constructive relations.

Iran's animosity toward Israel can be traced back to the founder of the republic, Ayatollah Ruhollah Khomeini. In his eyes, the unforgivable sin was the creation of a Jewish state in the Middle East. Iran's antagonism toward Israel exceeded even its opposition to the United States. After all, the United States may have been a pernicious imperial power, but it was America's conduct, not its right to exist, irrespective of its actual policies and behavior. No peace compact or negotiated settlement with the Palestinians could ameliorate that essential illegitimacy.

Iran's view of Israel, like its view of America, was religious defined, as a struggle between a pristine Islamic civilization and a blasphemous Zionist creed. In this conflict between good and evil, light and dark, it was religious obligation to resist the profane Jewish entity. The reclaiming of Jerusalem was not considered a Palestinian responsibility alone, but an obligation to be undertaken by the entire Muslim world. Such a conflict would lead not just to the destruction of Israel, but also to a greater Islamic cohesion and solidarity. It was natural, even inevitable, for the new Islamic regime in Iran to lead this crusade.

Iran's position on Israel has gone even beyond the Arab states and mainstream Palestinian organizations. For the past three decades, the Arab struggle has implicitly acknowledged the reality of Israel and has sought territorial concessions to establish a Palestinian homeland. Both terrorism and diplomacy have been employed to redraw the boundaries, but all such schemes appreciated the existence of Israel. The Iranian policy is designed not to readjust territorial demarcations, bit to evict the Jewish populace from the Middle East. The sacred land of Islam was not to be partitioned to accommodate Zionist aspirations, but reclaimed for the Muslim world.

Like many regimes in the Middle East, Iran has indulged in its share of historical revisionism. The infamous *Protocols of the Elders of Zion* has been routinely published by state agencies, while prominent Holocaust deniers are at times offered a platform in Iran for spewing their odious views. The Supreme Leader Ali Khamenei has even gone as far as to claim that "there are documents showing close collaboration of Zionists with Nazi Germany, and exaggerated numbers relating to the Jewish Holocaust were fabricated to solicit the sympathy of world public opinion, lay the ground for the occupation of Palestine, and justify the atrocities of the Zionists." In essence, Khamenei views the Holocaust as an embellished narrative to justify a Jewish homeland.

A similarly incendiary approach has characterized Tehran's attitude toward the ideology of Zionism. While Iran's clerical leaders may have sporadically displayed a benign attitude toward the local Jewish community, their condemnation of Zionism has been stark and uncompromising. To them, Zionism is a racist, exclusionary ideology that should be opposed by all who care about human rights, Iran's propaganda insists that Zionism was inflicted on the region by force of arms, sustained by bloodshed, and perpetuated by the sinister designs of cynical politicians inclined to achieve power by subjugating the indigenous population. The complex history of the Zionist movement and its claims and aspirations has been caricatured as fiery sermons and Jerusalem days and conferences calling for the annihilation of Israel replaced a rational assessment.

Over the past three decades, Iran has forged intimate ties with leading Palestinian militant groups such as Hamas and Islamic Jihad, as well as Lebanon's Hezbollah, which it essentially created. Iran has provided funds to these organizations, implored them to attack Israel and celebrated their terrorist operations. The leaders of these groups maintain representatives in Iran and have easy access to the theocratic state. No nation has suffered more at hands of Iran then Israel.

Toward New US Policy

The Islamic Republic's relentless expansionism stems in part from the belief that its revolution can be consolidated at home only if it is exported abroad. This was always, after all, a revolution without borders. Moreover, threats from the outside have always been a convenient way for the Revolutionary Guards and other state instruments to seek to justify their brutality. Thousands of executions since the revolution testify to the oppressive nature of the regime and to its overriding goal of shoring up its rule at home, particularly by eliminating the threat that emanates from its own people.

Today, the theocratic state is ruled by clerical ideologues who claim to know the mind of God. For them, the Islamic Republic is not merely a nation-state, it is a combatant in a struggle between good and evil, at home and abroad—a battle waged for moral redemption and genuine emancipation from the political and cultural tentacles of a profane West. The mullah's internationalist vision has to have an antagonist and the United States and its allies, particularly Israel, are it.

Still, in the 1990s, it looked as if the Islamic Republic would follow the trajectory of other revolutionary states and gradually dispense with its ideological patrimony. The rise of the reform movement led by enterprising intellectuals who sought to harmonize religious values with republican norms led to hopes of a different future. The election of Muhammad Khatami in 1997 was the culmination of efforts to connect the reformers to the larger public. The so-called Tehran Spring led to the rise of civil society groups, critical media and a string of electoral victories by leaders committed to genuine change. And then came the counter-reaction. Under the watchful eye of the Supreme Leader Ali Khamenei, the conservatives struck back. The clerical oversight bodies negated parliamentary legislation, the judiciary closed reformist newspapers and the vigilante groups assassinated key officials and terrorized others. To the detriment of the Islamic Republic, the possibility of evolutionary change through the use of Iran's own constitutional provisions died.

The starting point of any sensible policy is to recognize that the summer of 2009 was a watershed moment in the history of Iran. As we have seen, the presidential election that returned Mahmoud Ahmadinejad to power by rigging the vote presented the theocratic state with the most consequential crisis of its life-time. The Green Movement that exploded on the scene was a coalition of disenchanted clerics, restive youth, disenfranchised women and impoverished elements of the middle class. The regime managed to regain control of the streets through brutal violence against its own citizens, show trials in which regime loyalists confessed to fantastic crimes, and continued repression. However, the essential link between the state and society were severed. The Islamic Republic was never a typical totalitarian state, as its electoral procedures and elected institutions provided the public with at least impressions of democratic representation. That republican element of the regime provided it with a veneer of legitimacy—and in 2009 that legitimacy vanished. No less than Khamenei has acknowledged that the movement brought the system to the "edge of the cliff." The clerical regime lingers on, but a state that relies on a terror apparatus cannot forever stifle the forces of change.

The task of American diplomacy is similar to the one that Ronald Reagan faced with the Soviet Union: not just renegotiating a better arms-control agreement but devising a comprehensive policy that undermines the theocratic regime. In this regard, there is nothing as powerful as the presidential bully pulpit. Reagan's denunciations of Communist rule did much to galvanize the opposition and undermine the Soviet empire. Dissidents in jail and others laboring under the Soviet system took heart from an American president who championed their cause. Barrack Obama chose the opposite course and remained silent as protesters in 2009 called on America to support their cause. His administration was one that paid scant attention to Iran's human rights abuses.

As it did with Solidarity in Poland, the United States should find a way of establishing ties with forces of opposition within Iran. Given the Islamic Republic's cruelty and corruption, the opposition spans the entire social spectrum. The Iranians have given up not just on the Islamic Republic, but even on religious observance, as mosques go empty during most Shia commemorations. Three decades of theocratic rule has transformed Iran into one of the most secular nations in the world. The middle class and the working poor are equally hard pressed by the regime's incompetence and corruption. Even the senior ayatollahs are beginning to realize the toll that has taken on Shia Islam by its entanglement with politics. Americas has ready allies in Iran and must make an effort to empower those who share its values.

Economic sanctions are a critical aspect of any policy of pressuring the Islamic Republic. The experience of the past few years has shown that the United States has a real capacity to shrink Iran's economy and bring it to the brink of collapse. The fewer resources the regime has at its disposal, the less capable it is of sustaining a cadre whose loyalty is purchased. The guardians of the revolution are well aware of their unreliability of their coercive services; the government had difficulty in repressing the Green Movement or mobilizing counter-demonstrations in the summer of 2009. Designating the Revolutionary Guards as a terrorist organization and imposing financial sanctions could go a long way toward crippling Iran's economy. Once deprived of money, the mullahs will find it difficult to fund the patronage networks that are essential to their rule and their imperial ventures.

By generating such pressures, it is hoped that the Islamic Republic begins negotiating with the opposition elements. This will involve releasing political prisoners, allowing those barred from public service to stand as candidates for parliament, and ceasing its attacks on civil society groups such as trade unions and professional syndicates. The rulers of Iran will only embark on such activities if they are subject to sustained international pressure and condemnation. Iran should be held as accountable for its dismal human rights record, as its nuclear infractions or support for terrorism.

For the recalcitrant mullahs to yield to international norms, all the walls around them have to close in. So as it stresses Iran's economy and divides its society, the United States should also push back against its influence in the Middle East. By contesting Iran's gains, Washington can impose additional costs on the regime and contribute to regional stability. Iran's leaders believe that the vitality of their revolution mandates its export. And it is that export that must be jeopardized as means of undermining the revolution.

An essential insight of any such policy is to dispense with the false notion that Iran and America have a common enemy in the Islamic State (ISIS) or other Sunni terrorist organizations. Beneath Iran's expressions of concern about the rise of ISIS is a more cynical strategy. Iran today is using ISIS' ascendance in the Middle East to consolidate its power. The theocracy is now the key to keeping both Iraqi Shias and Alawite Bashar al-Assad's regime standing against well-armed and tenacious Sunni Jihadists. In those battles, Iran will do just enough to make sure the Sunnis don't conquer the Shia portions of Iraq and Assad's enclave in Syria, but no more. Meanwhile, in ISIS' wake, Tehran will strengthen its own Shia militias. It is important to stress the fact that Sunni radicalism is the necessary by-product of Iran's Shia chauvinism. Destroying the Islamic State requires diminishing the tides of Sunni militancy, which in turn necessitates tempering Iran's regional ambitions.

The best arena in which to achieve the objective of pushing back on Iran is in the Persian Gulf region. The Gulf sheikdoms, led by Saudi Arabia, are already locked into a region-wide rivalry with Iran. The Sunni states have taken it upon themselves to contest Iran's gains in the Gulf and the Levant. Washington should not only buttress these efforts but press all Arab states to embark on a serious attempt to lessen their commercial and diplomatic ties to Tehran. The price of American guardianship is for Sunni Arab states to do their part in resisting the rising Shia power of Iran.

Getting the Gulf states to agree to take common action has always been difficult. The United States should help the Gulf states no only as they battle Iranian proxies in Syria, Iraq and Yemen, but also as they deal with a range of other challenges. These include protecting themselves against Iran's efforts to undermine their internal security, defending their economic infrastructure (such as oil and gas platforms, water-desalinization plants, and tourist sites), and preventing Iran from interdicting their energy exports along key transit routes.

To confront Iran, the Gulf states will need capabilities commensurate with the challenge. In particular, the United States should consider supplying them with systems that defend against guided rockets and mortars, such as the Centurion c-ram. And in the long-run, the Gulf states have the financial resources, even at reduced oil prices, to invest in the next generation of missile defense technologies, such as directed-energy weapons, which would diminish Iran's ability to attack them.

The countries in the region with formidable special-forces capabilities, such as Jordan and the United Arab Emirates, should use that advantage to help some of the more vulnerable countries, such as Bahrain, deal with their internal security problems—arrangements that Washington could help broker. Iran's adversaries could even develop a subset of special forces capable of operating inside Iran to exploit the grievances of various ethnic minorities. The goal would be to make Iran think twice about its campaign of regional subversion by demonstrating that two can play that game.

The Gulf states need to further reduce Iran's ability to chock off oil exports by blocking the Strait of Hormuz. Although they have already built pipelines to bypass the strait, they should also take steps to increase those pipelines capacity. The Gulf states should invest in capabilities such as air-to-air missiles to take down Iran's aircraft and land-attack cruise missiles to destroy its anti-ship cruise missiles. And they should augment that effort with the undersea capabilities needed for a campaign against Iran's surface naval assets, including its many small boats.

Even in a disorderly Middle East, there are opportunities to forge new constructive alliances. The enmity that Saudi Arabia and Israel share toward Iran should be the basis for bringing these two countries closer together. Instead of lecturing the Saudis to share the Middle East with Iran and hectoring Israelis about settlements, the United Should focus on imaginative ways of institutionalizing the nascent cooperation that is already taking place between Riyadh and Jerusalem. The U.S. should press both countries to move beyond intelligence sharing and perhaps force complementary trade ties, with Saudi oil exchanged for Israeli technological products. History rarely offers opportunities to realign the politics of the Middle East: a truculent Iran has presented this chance.

Another alliance that needs refurbishing after years of neglect and rancor, is the US-Israeli relationship. One of the most spurious yet pervasive arguments has been that America's ties with Israel damages its standing in the Middle East. To be effective in the Middle East, it is claimed, Washington should put some distance between itself and the only democracy in the region. Any strategy of pushing back on Iran has to have Israel as one of its core elements. The fact is that the Islamic Republic respects Israeli power and fears its integration in the Middle East. An Israel closely tied to the United States enhances our deterrent power. And an Israel that is mending fences with Sunni Arab states only empowers the anti-Iran alliance and further isolates the theocracy in the region. America's task should not be to distant itself from Israel but to bring all elements of its anti-Iran coalition together.

Although today Iraq seems like a protectorate of Iran, this is a predicament that most Iraqi leaders want to escape. Iraq was once the seat of Arab civilization and the center of the region's politics. The Shia leaders in Iraq take Iranian advice and money for the simple reason that they are locked out of Sunni Arab councils and abandoned by the American superpower. Iraqis understand that Iran has exercised a pernicious influence in their country, further accentuating its sectarian divides as a means of ensuring Iranian influence. Iraq cannot be whole and free so long as Iran interferes in its affairs. A commitment by the United States to once more rehabilitate Iraqi army and bureaucracy can go a long way toward diminishing its ties to Tehran. No Iraqi Arab wants to be subordinate to imperious Shia Persians. Once Iraq fees itself of Iranian dominance, it may yet find a path back to the Arab world and once more serve as a barrier to Iranian power.

At a practical level, Washington should also push Baghdad to govern more inclusively, so that the central government is seen as benefiting Sunnis and Kurds, and just the Shias. It should make an outreach to the Sunni tribes on a scale equivalent to what took place during the 2007 surge of U.S. troops. And it should ramp up its military assistance to Kurds and the Sunni tribal forces, intensify the air campaign against ISIS in both Iraq and Syria, and embed U.S. personnel in the Iraqi military at lower levels than it currently does. A heightened U.S. presence in Iraq need not entail a massive combat force there, but it would mean a larger troop presence and thus a greater risk of casualties. Again, the price for greater U.S. involvement should be a commitment on the part of local actors to press back against Tehran and its enablers.

The tragedy of Syria is that, as the Obama administration stood aloof and preoccupied itself with useless international summits, Iran and Russia possibly succeeded in saving the Assad Dynasty. The Syrian army, buttressed by Iran's Revolutionary Guards, Hezbollah terrorists, and Russian airpower, is poised to control most of the population centers. This hardly ends the civil war, but the attempt to unseat Iran's client in Damascus will take considerable effort and commitment by the United States and its Sunni allies. For both strategic and humanitarian reasons, we should embrace this task. Pushing back on Iran means harassing its Syrian proxy. At the very least, as the opposition strengthens, Iran will have to face the dilemma of sinking more resources and men into a quagmire or cutting its losses, as the Soviet Union was forced to do in Afghanistan.

As regime as dangerous to U.S. interest as the Islamic Republic requires a comprehensive strategy to counter it. This means exploiting all of Iran's vulnerabilities; increasing the costs of its foreign adventures, weakening its economy, and supporting its domestic discontents. Pursuing that strategy will take time, but eventually, it will put the United States in a position to impose terms on Iran. We should not settle for an arms control agreement that paves the way for an Iranian bomb, but a restrictive accord that ends its nuclear weapons aspirations. We should seek to compel Iran to cease its regional subversion, not create power vacuums that encourage it. And we should move human rights up the agenda, not look the other way as Iran's leaders oppress their people.

Some in Washington believe that Iran problem is of secondary importance to the United States compared to violent Jihadists. For all their achievements, those radical movements do not yet possess the resources and capabilities of a large, sophisticated state. It must be noted that the Iranian regime was the original Islamic revolutionary state. Its successes inspired a wave of radicals across the Middle East. At its most basic level, the confrontation between the United States and Iran is a conflict between the world's sole superpower and a second-rate autocracy. Washington does not need to settle for hopes that theocrats with no interest in relaxing their grip will somehow become moderates. A determined policy of pressure would speed the day when the Iranian people replace a regime that has made their lives miserable. And in the interim, it would reduce the threat of a triumphant regime posed to the Middle East and the world beyond.

In the end, the nuclear agreement offered Iran all that it wanted. The accord conceded a vast enrichment capability, as well as accepting both a heavy water plant and a well-fortified underground enrichment facility that the United States once vowed to shutter. It permitted an elaborate research and development program while relying on an inspection regime that falls short of the indispensable "anytime, anywhere" access. In the meantime, the sanctions architecture is diminished, and the notion of ever "snapping back" sanctions into place once they are lifted is delusional. And the financial dividends of the agreement have once more revived Iran's imperialist dreams in the Middle East.

Mr. POE. Dr. Byman.

STATEMENT OF DANIEL L. BYMAN, PH.D., SENIOR FELLOW, CENTER FOR MIDDLE EAST POLICY, BROOKINGS INSTITUTION

Mr. BYMAN. Thank you, Mr. Chairman. I will try to emulate Dr. Takeyh.

Mr. Chairman, Mr. Keating, members of this subcommittee, thank you very much for this opportunity to testify.

Iran's terrorism and destabilization efforts are primarily a threat to U.S. interests and U.S. allies in the Middle East. Support for militant and terrorist groups in Iraq, Syria, Yemen, and elsewhere enable Tehran to show up key allies like the Syrian regime, Bashar al-Assad. It also gives Iran leverage with regional rivals like Saudi Arabia. And ties to militant groups strengthen pro-Iran voices in the region, increasing Iran's influence in some of the capitals in the region, but also in some of the more remote hinterlands. Iran believes that support for militants pays policy dividends.

The Assad regime, once teetering, is now ascendant or at least in a stronger position. Iran's support to various groups in Iraq have given Tehran influence at both the local and national level. And Hezbollah has proven a loyal ally that has helped Iran project its influence in Lebanon and in neighboring states and against Israel. Iran does not appear to be actively targeting the U.S. homeland with terrorism, but its capacity remains latent. Tehran uses its ability to strike U.S. assets outside war zones to deter the United States and as a contingency should the United States attack Iran. Iran spends billions of dollars on supporting its proxies and de- ploying its own military forces. This is a huge sum for a country with significant economic problems and a limited military budget. In addition, the nuclear deal raised expectations of economic im- provements among the Iranian people, and spending more on mili- tants abroad makes it harder for the regime to satisfy these demands at home.

For the Trump administration to better counter Iranian influence in the Middle East, it should seize the opportunity to reset U.S. relations with key regional allies. Many Middle Eastern allies had lost faith in the Obama administration, and several, notably Israel and Saudi Arabia, are going to elaborate lengths to ignore the missteps and often contradictory behavior of the Trump administration in hopes of closer cooperation. Additional pressure on entities like the Islamic Revolutionary Guard Corps would help send the right message to allies and to Iran. Washington should also highlight the cost of Iran's adventurism to ordinary Iranians to raise domestic awareness and discontent with the regime's foreign policy.

The United States should step up efforts to build a credible and modern Syrian opposition to put additional pressure on Iran's Syrian ally. And in Yemen, Washington should support negotiations to end the war, as the current Saudi approach is giving both Iran and the al-Qaeda affiliate in Yemen an opportunity to expand their influence.

At the same time, the Trump administration must remember that Iran can push back. The 2015 nuclear deal, for all its flaws, remains better than any current plausible alternative, and pulling out of the agreement would be a mistake. In addition, Iran has leverage and many vulnerabilities to exploit, given its role in fighting the Islamic State and the exposure of U.S. troops in Iraq and Syria to Iranian-directed violence.

Mr. Chairman, thank you, again, for this opportunity to testify.

[The prepared statement of Mr. Byman follows:]

Nuclear Deal Fallout: The Global Threat of Iran

Prepared Testimony of Daniel Byman

Professor, Edmund A. Walsh School of Foreign Service at Georgetown University

Senior Fellow, Center for Middle East Policy at the Brookings Institution

House Committee on Foreign Affairs
Subcommittee on Terrorism, Nonproliferation, and Trade

May 24, 2017

Chairman Poe, Ranking Member Keating, members of this distinguished subcommittee, and subcommittee staff, thank you for the opportunity to testify.

Relationships with terrorist and militant groups are integral to Iran's foreign policy. The clerical regime in Tehran sponsors a range of organizations in the Middle East and maintains the capacity to conduct international terrorism outside the region. Iran's terrorism and destabilization efforts are primarily a threat to U.S. interests and allies in the Middle East: Tehran's activities worsen civil wars and contribute to the destabilization of the region. Iran does not appear to be actively targeting the U.S. homeland with terrorism, but its capacity remains latent. Tehran uses its ability to strike U.S. assets outside war zones to deter the United States and as a contingency should the United States attack Iran.

Support for militant and terrorist groups in Iraq, Syria, Yemen, and elsewhere benefits Iran in several ways. It enables Tehran to shore up key allies like the Syrian regime of Bashar al-Asad. It also gives Iran leverage against regional rivals like Saudi Arabia. Ties to militant groups strengthen pro-Iran voices in the region, increasing Iran's influence in some capitals and in the more remote hinterlands of several countries. Finally, the threat of Iranian terrorism against otherwise stable countries is a factor these countries must consider if they choose to confront Tehran.

For the Trump administration to better counter Iranian influence in the Middle East, it should seize the opportunity to reset U.S. relations with key regional allies. Many Middle Eastern allies had lost faith in the Obama administration and several, notably Israel and Saudi Arabia, are going to elaborate lengths to ignore the missteps and often contradictory behavior of the Trump administration in the hopes of closer cooperation. Additional pressure on entities like the Islamic Revolutionary Guard Corps would help send the right message to allies and to Iran. Washington should also highlight the costs of Iran's adventurism to ordinary Iranians to raise domestic awareness of, and discontent with, the regime's foreign policy. The United States should step up its efforts to build a credible and moderate Syrian opposition, putting additional pressure on Iran's Syrian ally. In Yemen, Washington should support negotiations to end the war as the current Saudi approach is giving both Iran and the Al Qaeda affiliate in Yemen opportunities to expand their influence.

At the same time, the Trump administration must remember the limits of U.S. power and Iran's ability to push back. The 2015 Joint Comprehensive Plan of Action (JCPOA), for all its flaws, remains better than any current plausible alternatives, and pulling out of the agreement would be a mistake. In general, Iran's use of militant groups is well-entrenched: a successful policy would reduce the scope and scale of Iranian support but not end it. In addition, Iran has leverage and many vulnerabilities to exploit given its role in fighting the Islamic State and the exposure of U.S. troops in Iraq and Syria to Iranian-directed violence.

My statement first details Iran's motivations for supporting militant and terrorist groups, with an emphasis on Iraq, Syria, and Yemen. I then discuss the threat to the United States, both directly and indirectly. I argue that Iran's overall stance toward militant groups is not likely to change in the near-term. I conclude by offering policy recommendations for the Trump administration.[1]

Iran's Motivations for Supporting Terrorist and Militant Groups

Iran has supported terrorist and militant groups in the Islamic world since the 1979 revolution. In his 2016 testimony, Director of National Intelligence (DNI) James Clapper warned: "Iran—the foremost state sponsor of terrorism—continues to exert its influence in regional crises in the Middle East through the Islamic Revolutionary Guard Corps—Qods Force (IRGC-QF), its terrorist partner Lebanese Hizballah, and proxy groups" – an assessment that has stayed roughly constant for many years.[2]

Iran has long sought to "try hard to export our revolution to the world," in the words of Ayatollah Khomeini, the clerical regime's dominant revolutionary leader.[3] This goal is embedded in Iran's constitution and in the missions of organizations such as the Islamic Revolutionary Guard Corps (IRGC), a military and paramilitary organization that oversees Iran's relationships with many substate groups.

Revolutionary ideology, however, has long taken a backseat to more strategic goals. In the decades since the 1979 revolution, Iran has used terrorism and support for militant groups to undermine and bleed rivals, intimidate the Gulf states and other

---

[1] This testimony draws in part on two of my books: *Deadly Connections: States that Sponsor Terrorism* (Cambridge: Cambridge University Press, 2005) and *A High Price: The Triumphs and Failures of Israeli Counterterrorism* (Oxford: Oxford University Press, 2011). Also relevant to my testimony and to this hearing are my articles, "Iran, Terrorism, and Weapons of Mass Destruction," *Studies in Conflict and Terrorism* 31, no. 3 (2008): 169-181; "The Lebanese Hizballah and Israeli Counterterrorism," *Studies in Conflict and Terrorism* 34, no. 12 (2011): 917-941; and Daniel Byman and Bilal Saab, "Hezbollah Hesitates?" *Foreign Affairs*, January 21, 2015, https://www.foreignaffairs.com/articles/israel/2015-01-21/hezbollah-hesitates.

[2] James Clapper, *Worldwide Threat Assessment of the U.S. Intelligence Community: Statement for the Record for the Senate Armed Services Committee* (February 9, 2016): 6, https://www.armed-services.senate.gov/imo/media/doc/Clapper_02-09-16.pdf.

[3] As quoted in Anoushiravan Ehteshami, *After Khomeini: The Iranian Second Republic* (New York: Routledge, 1995), 131.

neighbors, project power to make itself a player in the Israeli-Palestinian dispute and other arenas, disrupt peace negotiations that might isolate Iran and benefit Israel, and deter enemies, including the United States, that might otherwise use force against it. Iran has also sponsored terrorist attacks to take vengeance on countries that have supported its enemies, hosted its dissidents, or killed its operatives.

Finally, as a relatively weak state with hostile neighbors, Iran maintains ties to violent groups for contingencies, strengthening the relationship as need be depending on changing circumstances. Given Iran's considerable success in spreading its influence in the Middle East and hostility to the United States and its allies, many observers often overrate its power. Iran's conventional military is weak, and its economy, while beginning to improve, remains in poor shape. Ties to terrorist and militant groups is a relatively cheap way for Iran to offset its weaknesses.

Because Iran works through terrorist and militant groups, it gains a degree of deniability for some of its actions. This deniability, however, is better characterized as willing disbelief on the part of many countries rather than true uncertainty. If a group like the Lebanese Hizballah carries out an attack, observers may debate whether Iran gave the order. However, the broader Iranian policy that facilitates and supports such attacks is rarely in question. The depth of Iran's ties, the shared goals between Iran and many proxies, the clerical regime's long history of association with violent groups, and the fact that many past instances of terrorism showed involvement of individuals at or near the top of Iran's hierarchy should lead observers to err on the side of Iranian responsibility.

Current Iranian Activities: A Brief Review

Tehran's closest militant ally is the **Lebanese Hizballah**, perhaps the most capable terrorist group in the world. Iran helped create Hizballah in the early 1980s, and in subsequent decades has armed, trained, and otherwise nurtured it. This assistance is massive: Iran regularly gave Hizballah over $100 million a year, and in many years the figure is significantly higher. Iran's military aid includes relatively advanced weaponry, such as anti-tank and anti-ship cruise missiles, as well as thousands of rockets and artillery systems. Hizballah has emerged as a key bulwark of the Syrian regime, and Hizballah operatives work with Iran globally to prepare and conduct terrorist attacks.[4]

Tehran has long worked with **Palestinian groups**. Relations are especially close to Palestine Islamic Jihad, though these ties discredited the group among many Palestinians. Tehran has also had extensive ties to Hamas at different times in the group's history, though their fallout over the Syrian and Yemeni civil wars lead to a decline in funding and military aid and frayed, but did not end, relations in general. In 2016, however, the pragmatic Hamas again resumed its public praise for Iran, in part because the coup in Egypt deprived Hamas of a key ally and because by then revolution in Syria looked less likely.[5] Iran, unlike other states, was willing to offer Hamas serious weaponry as well as funding.

---

[4] For a review of Hizballah's international agenda, see Matthew Levitt, *Hezbollah: The Global Footprint of Lebanon's Party of God* (Washington, DC: Georgetown University Press, 2013).

[5] Hazem Balousha, "Why Hamas Resumed Relations with Iran," June 29, 2016, *Al-Monitor*, http://www.al-monitor.com/pulse/originals/2016/06/gaza-hamas-resume-relations-iran.html.

In **Iraq,** Iran has played an influential role since the toppling of Saddam Hussein's regime in 2003. Iran has close ties to the Haider al-Abadi government in Baghdad, but its goals differ from those of its Iraqi partners. Iran wants a state that is weak and vulnerable to its influence, while Iraqi leaders seek a strong regime and country. In addition to relations with the Abadi administration, Iran maintains influence by supporting a host of militant groups, particularly within the Hashd al-Shaabi (or Popular Mobilization Forces), an umbrella militia organization that is playing a leading role in pushing the Islamic State out of Iraq.[6] Many preexisting Shi'a militias supported (and even created) by Iran, such as the Badr Organization, Asa'ib Ahl al-Haq, and Kata'ib Hizballah, joined the Hashd al-Shaabi, thus gaining greater popular legitimacy, combat experience, and state recognition. Iran gives these groups, which number perhaps 100,000 in total, money, arms, training, and other forms of assistance. Through these ties, Iran exercises influence is both at the national level in Iraq and at the local level.

In **Syria,** Tehran is the chief patron of the regime of Bashar al-Asad, and without Iran's help it is likely the regime would have fallen by now. Iran has long seen the Syrian regime as a vital ally – it is Tehran's only true state ally in the Arab world, and perhaps even in the entire world. To save the Syrian regime, Iran has deployed several thousand IRGC and regular army forces,[7] and Iran also commands another 25,000 or so foreign Shi'a fighters from Afghanistan, Iraq, Lebanon, and Pakistan.[8] Regime forces number perhaps 250,000 in total, counting both regular and irregular forces, so Iranian-supported foreigners represent at least 10 percent of the total and an even larger percentage of the forces on which the regime can truly rely.[9]

Iran arms, trains, and funds these foreign fighters. Quasi-government foundations in Iran also provide financial support for the wounded and the families of the slain. In Syria, Iranian officers often command these fighters (as they also do for many Syrian groups), and Iran works with Syria to provide logistical support.[10] The foreign fighters have played a role in almost every aspect of combat, helping guard key areas, storm cities, and shore up Syrian regular army forces.

Hizballah in particular has played critical roles in battles for Qusayr, Damascus, Aleppo, and other cities, bolstering Syrian government forces and providing key shock

---

[6] Priyanka Boghani, "Iraq's Shia Militias: The Double-Edged Sword against ISIS," *Frontline*, March 21, 2017, http://www.pbs.org/wgbh/frontline/article/iraqs-shia-militias-the-double-edged-sword-against-isis/.

[7] See Paul Bucala, "Iran's New Way of War in Syria," *Institute for the Study of War*, February 2017, http://www.understandingwar.org/sites/default/files/Iran%20New%20Way%20of%20War%20in%20Syria_FEB%202017.pdf.

[8] Farzin Nadimi, "Iran's Afghan and Pakistan Proxies: In Syria and Beyond?" *Washington Institute*, August 22, 2016, http://www.washingtoninstitute.org/policy-analysis/view/irans-afghan-and-pakistani-proxies-in-syria-and-beyond; Hashmatallah Moslih, "Iran 'foreign legion' leans on Afghan Shia in Syria War," *Al Jazeera*, January 22, 2016, http://www.aljazeera.com/news/2016/01/iran-foreign-legion-leans-afghan-shia-syria-war-160122130355206.html. Nadimi gives the figure of 14,000 Afghan forces and 5,000 Pakistani forces, whereas Moslih gives the figure of 20,000. For the Afghan fighters, the numbers include significant numbers of Afghan refugees whose families live in Iran. See also: Cody Roche, "Assad Regime Militias and Shi'ite Jihadis in the Syrian Civil War," *Bellingcat*, November 30, 2016, https://www.bellingcat.com/news/mena/2016/11/30/assad-regime-militias-and-shiite-jihadis-in-the-syrian-civil-war/; Phillip Smyth, *The Shiite Jihad in Syria*. (Washington Institute, February 2015): 41, https://www.washingtoninstitute.org/uploads/Documents/pubs/PolicyFocus138_Smyth-2.pdf.

[9] Roche, "Assad Regime Militias and Shi'ite Jihadis in the Syrian Civil War."

[10] Nadimi, "Iran's Afghan and Pakistan Proxies."

troops when necessary.[11] The intervention has come at a high cost for Hizballah—an estimated 1,500-2,000 dead and many thousands more wounded, which are significant numbers for the relatively small group.[12] The Syria conflict has also forced Hizballah to devote less attention and resources to its traditional adversary, Israel. In addition, the conflict is exhausting for the Lebanese Shi'a and may make Hizballah more cautious in the future. However, as much as the war has been a serious strain on the organization and its personnel, it has also provided valuable combat experience, greater access to weapons and technology, and, through Russia, an education in conventional maneuver warfare.[13]

In addition to giving the Syrian regime more combat power, using proxies from Afghanistan, Iraq, and Pakistan to fight in Syria will have the long-term impact of increasing Iran's influence in these countries in years to come. When these fighters return, they will have organizational and personal ties to Iranian leaders. In addition, their increased military power will make them more important local actors, helping their communities but also Iran.

In **Yemen,** Iran provides small arms to Houthi forces, and the use of anti-ship cruise missiles against U.S. and Emirati warships suggests greater Iranian investment as well as technical training and assistance. However, there is little publically available evidence of any significant personnel presence.[14] In contrast to Iran's presence in Iraq and Syria, Yemen is not a strategic priority for Tehran, and it is probably using its support for the Houthis as a way to gain leverage against the UAE and Saudi Arabia, drain their attention (and coffers), and counter what it perceives as the Gulf states' aggressive stance against it.

Because Iran's approach is more strategic than ideological, it is willing to work tactically with groups like **Al Qaeda**, even though mutual mistrust limits cooperation. Iran has at times allowed Sunni jihadists to transit Iran and given Al Qaeda operatives a de facto safe haven, albeit one that Al Qaeda has contended is restrictive.[15]

Iran's partnering with various Shi'a and minority groups in the Middle East has worsened the sectarian climate, made existing civil wars bloodier, and contributed to a back and forth with Saudi Arabia and other Sunni states that further ratchets up regional tension. For Sunni states, Iran's support to militant groups is proof that the clerical regime is bent on spreading its revolution and that it supports subversive activities in their own countries. Iran, however, sees itself as an "Islamic" actor, not a Shi'a power, and often works with Shi'a groups by default because few Sunni groups are willing to ally with it – an approach that increases its isolation from the Sunni powers.

[11] Mona Alami, "Hezbollah Embedded in Syria," *Atlantic Council*, March 2, 2017, http://www.atlanticcouncil.org/blogs/syriasource/hezbollah-is-embedded-in-syria.

[12] Mona Alami, "After Aleppo victory, what's next for Hezbollah?" *Al-Monitor*, January 24, 2017, http://www.al-monitor.com/pulse/originals/2017/01/hezbollah-syria-aleppo-victory-role-lebanon.html.

[13] Muni Katz and Nadav Pollak, "Hezbollah's Russian Military Education in Syria," *Washington Institute*, December 24, 2015, http://www.washingtoninstitute.org/policy-analysis/view/hezbollahs-russian-military-education-in-syria.

[14] Sam LaGrone, "USS Mason Fired 3 Missiles to Defend from Yemen Cruise Missile Attack," *USNI News*, October 11, 2016, https://news.usni.org/2016/10/11/uss-mason-fired-3-missiles-to-defend-from-yemen-cruise-missiles-attack.

[15] Al Qaeda impressions of the relationship with Iran can be found in Nelly Lahoud et al., "Letters from Abbottabad: Bin Ladin Sidelined?" *Combating Terrorism Center at West Point* May 3, 2012, http://www.ctc.usma.edu/posts/letters-fromabbottabad-bin-ladin-sidelined.

Most of Iran's efforts against Israel involve aiding proxies such as Hizballah or assisting groups like Hamas to fight Israel. The killing of Iranian scientists before the JCPOA, which Tehran blamed on Israel, and Israel's killing of key operatives also fostered a desire for revenge, which Iran has attempted to take through terrorist attacks.

The Implications of Iran's Actions for the United States

Iran's use of extra-regional terrorism directly against the United States appears to have declined since negotiations over Iran's nuclear program began in earnest. Iran has not repeated any plot similar to the 2011 plot on the Saudi ambassador to the United States. DNI Clapper's public testimony in 2016 stressed the danger Iran's terrorism posed to U.S. allies and interests, not the U.S. homeland.

However, Iran probably has at least some capacity to use terrorism to strike the U.S. homeland and almost certainly has the ability to strike U.S. assets around the world. Iranian leaders probably fear any strike would create a dangerous escalation with the United States. Nevertheless, they want to maintain the capacity as a possible deterrent to increases in U.S. pressure and especially direct U.S. military action against Tehran.

A military strike by Israel or the United States on Iran would probably prompt a more massive terrorism response. Tehran backs terrorist groups in part to keep its options open: after a U.S. strike, it would call in its chits. Iran would probably attempt terrorist attacks around the world, using its own operatives, the Lebanese Hizballah, and other groups. Tehran would also step up militant activity against U.S. forces in Afghanistan, Syria, and Iraq, using its proxies and perhaps its own paramilitary forces to conduct attacks. The scope and scale of the Iranian response would depend on the level of casualties from the initial attack against it as well as the political circumstances of the regime in Tehran (and those of strong groups like Hizballah) at the time the attack occurred.

Iran's support for the Iraqi government and other forces fighting against the Islamic State adds a further degree of complexity to U.S. efforts to diminish Iran's influence. Iran-backed forces in Iraq have proven effective, often far more so than the Iraqi government. Although U.S. officials contend that there is no formal cooperation between U.S. forces and the IRGC or Hizballah, the United States does coordinate with the Lebanese government and especially the Iraqi government – and both of these coordinate with Iran and have militaries and security forces that Iranian intelligence has probably penetrated extensively. So de facto coordination, or at least deconfliction of operations, is likely occurring.

Successes against the Islamic State in the last two years are posing additional challenges regarding the Iranian role. Many Shi'a militias claim they will resist any lasting U.S. presence in Iraq.[16] This would represent a serious security challenge as the Iraqi Security Forces cannot be expected, either militarily or politically, to effectively protect U.S. forces or defeat remnants of the Islamic State without U.S. assistance.

If the United States targets IRGC forces in Syria or that of its proxies, they might strike back against U.S. forces in Syria and elsewhere in the region. If the United States

---

[16] Rikar Hussein and Mehdi Jedinia, "Shi'ite Militias Could Turn against U.S. Forces after IS Leaves Mosul," *Voice of America News,* March 23, 2017, http://www.voanews.com/a/shiite-militias-could-turn-against-us-forces-after-is-leaves-mosul/3779207.html.

more aggressively targets the Syrian regime, there is greater potential for conflict with Iran, especially if Tehran believes the United States is playing a significant role and is likely to maintain this role until the Syrian regime falls.

Support for Militant Groups Likely to Continue

Iran is likely to continue to put support for militant groups at the front and center of its foreign policy, but Tehran also faces problems should it seek to significantly increase its support for radical groups.

Iran can sustain its high levels of support. In April 2017, the World Bank reported Iran's economy did well in 2016 due to sanctions relief facilitated by the JCPOA. This economic relief has in turn certainly helped Iran sustain its regional military activities, proxy support, and weapons development.[17] In addition, Iran believes support for militants pays policy dividends. The Asad regime, once teetering, is now ascendant or at least in a stronger position. Iran's support to various groups in Iraq have given Tehran influence at both the local and national level. Hizballah has proven a loyal ally that has helped Iran project its influence in Lebanon and in neighboring states.

Although some look to the recent election in Iran and hope for dramatic changes, this is not likely though halting progress is possible. President Rouhani, an early leader of Iranian intelligence and a member of the regime's elite, is committed to Iran's political system. However, he is a pragmatist who recognizes that Iran's economic weakness and political isolation hinder its government and is thus willing to make concessions to alleviate these conditions. Rouhani's priorities are economic and social, not diplomatic: he believes that the JCPOA and a less aggressive foreign policy will increase international investment and lead to an end of sanctions, enabling Iran's economy to flourish. Rouhani as president is better than the alternative of a clerical regime ideologue, but there should be no illusions. In addition, much of Iran's support for terrorist and militant groups is controlled by the IRGC and other more aggressive elements of the regime.

Fortunately, Hizballah at this point is leery of any escalation against Israel despite its continuing enmity. Because Hizballah's forces are deeply engaged in the draining war in Syria – a war that also decreased Hizballah's popularity among non-Shi'a in Lebanon and the broader Arab world – it is overstretched, and it would be difficult for the group to sustain several large wars at once. Since the 2006 war with Israel, Hizballah has been cautious in how it has approached Israel, and it respects Israel's formidable military. Hizballah's leaders also know that renewed conflict would lead to a devastating Israeli response in Lebanon, which might further decrease Hizballah's popularity there.

The cost of Iran's support is considerable though difficult to judge from unclassified sources. Iran spends billions of dollars on supporting its proxies and deploying its own military forces – a huge sum for a country with significant economic problems and a limited military budget.[18] In addition, the JCPOA raised expectations of

---

[17] The World Bank, "Iran's Economic Outlook," (April 2017), http://www.worldbank.org/en/country/iran/publication/economic-outlook-april-2017.

[18] For open estimates based on unclassified sources, see Karim El-Bar, "Proxies and Politics: Why Iran Funds Foreign Militias," *Middle East Eye*, October 6, 2016, http://www.middleeasteye.net/essays/proxies-and-politics-why-iran-funds-foreign-militias-2124504867. See also Eli Lake, "Iran Spends Billions to Prop

economic improvement among the Iranian people, and spending more on militants abroad makes it harder for the regime to satisfy these demands at home.

Iran's considerable economic mismanagement also limits its power. The World Bank also reported that Iran's oil production is nearing capacity and that continuing sanctions are inhibiting Iran's reintegration into international financial markets.[19] Despite the economic benefits gained from the JCPOA, unemployment, especially youth unemployment, remains high. Many among the regime, including the Supreme Leader, seek a "resistance economy," an approach that will diminish Iran's dependence on international markets but, in so doing, hinder economic prosperity in general.[20]

Policy Implications and Recommendations for the Trump Administration

Because the Islamic State has suffered significant reverses in the last two years, Iran is emerging as more of a priority for the United States in the Middle East. The Trump administration has yet to articulate a coherent Iran or Middle East strategy, although the President's remarks in his trip to Saudi Arabia and Israel suggest Iran may be the focus of his administration's regional policies. The Trump administration's rhetoric is aggressive, but it has largely continued to follow the policies of the last administration and has signed off on sanctions waivers.[21]

The Trump administration appears to view Iran's challenges more broadly than did Obama's administration. They see the flaws rather than the benefits of the JCPOA and emphasize Iran's support for militant groups and other dangerous activities.[22] Because the JCPOA, for now at least, has put Iran's nuclear program on the back burner, there is an opportunity to focus on Iran's support for militant groups and other problems Iran causes in the region.

The Trump administration has an opportunity to reinvigorate U.S. alliances in the Middle East. Saudi Arabia and other key allies split with the Obama administration over the Iran deal, U.S. support for several of the Arab Spring revolutions, the U.S. reluctance to engage in Syria, and other issues. As the warm Saudi reception of President Trump indicates, they are hoping for a closer relationship, especially given the Trump administration's signals that it is comfortable embracing dictators and does not favor incorporating human rights into U.S. diplomacy.

In addition to developing closer relations with allies, the Trump administration should highlight the cost of Iran's support for Asad, Hizballah, and other organizations to ordinary Iranians, making it clear to the Iranian public that their economic suffering is

Up Assad," June 9, 2015, https://www.bloomberg.com/view/articles/2015-06-09/iran-spends-billions-to-prop-up-assad

[19] The World Bank, "Iran's Economic Outlook."

[20] Rohollah Faghihi, "Iran's supreme leader calls for 'economy of resistance' in Nowruz message," *Al-Monitor*, March 20, 2017, http://www.al-monitor.com/pulse/originals/2017/03/iran-nowruz-video-message-khamenei-rouhani-2017-1396.html.

[21] See, for example, Elise Labott and Nicole Gaouette, "Trump adds to tough talk on Iran even as he sticks with deal – for now," *CNN*, April 20, 2017, http://www.cnn.com/2017/04/19/politics/tillerson-iran-nuclear-deal-review/.

[22] Suzanne Maloney, "Under Trump, U.S. policy is moving from accommodation to confrontation," *Markaz blog*, May 11, 2017, https://www.brookings.edu/blog/markaz/2017/05/11/under-trump-u-s-policy-on-iran-is-moving-from-accommodation-to-confrontation/.

linked to Iran's aggressive foreign policy. The depth of Iranian popular support for these groups is not clear, and the United States should try to increase the domestic price for Iran's aggressive foreign policy. Washington should also shine a spotlight on Tehran's ties to Al Qaeda and other Sunni jihadist groups. Such a relationship is embarrassing to both Tehran and the Sunni jihadists, and an information campaign could harm this cooperation and further discredit both.

The Trump administration should also lay down clear "red lines" regarding Iran's support for militant groups. Particularly important lines include the transfer of unconventional weapons to a terrorist group or any strike on the U.S. homeland or U.S. facilities abroad. Administration officials, in consultation with Congressional leaders, should decide in advance where the red lines are and what would happen if a red line were crossed. They must also have the will and ability to follow through on the response should this happen. During both the George W. Bush and Obama administrations, Tehran repeatedly crossed U.S. red lines in Iraq and Afghanistan with relatively few consequences, reducing the credibility of future U.S. threats. If the United States is not serious about a response, it is better not to threaten at all.

Although I do not favor designating the Islamic Revolutionary Guard Corps a terrorist group for technical reasons (as a state actor, it does not belong in the non-state category we use for terrorism), I favor similar or identical sanctions on it, perhaps using Executive Order 13224.[23] I would urge Congress to grant the President authority to punish the IRGC, amending legislation related to state sponsorship of terrorism as appropriate. In addition to supporting terrorist and militant groups, the IRGC has historically been used to crush anti-revolutionary forces at home and quell restive minorities.[24]

To counter Iran's influence in the Middle East, the United States should also step up support for anti-Asad opposition forces in Syria, particularly those from the Sunni Muslim community. Greater support would give the United States more credibility with its regional allies and would help the United States push back against Iran's ally Syria as well as the Islamic State. It would also provide the United States and its allies more options in a future Syria. Efforts to substitute U.S. forces for local forces, however, are likely to create power vacuums that Iran or other hostile actors might exploit.

Any substantial new initiative or form of pressure is going to require allies. Economic pressure requires support from European and Asian allies, while military and diplomatic pressure requires Middle Eastern help as well.

Another important diplomatic option is to encourage U.S. allies in the Arab world to improve their relationships with the Iraqi government. Baghdad works with Tehran in part because it has few other potential partners in the Middle East. Many Iraqis, including some Iraqi Shi'a, chafe at Tehran's dominant influence in their country and embrace their Arab identity. Integrating Iraq further into the Arab world will also help Baghdad win over Iraqi Sunnis and hinder future Islamic State recruiting efforts.

---

[23] For this proposal to use Executive Order 13224, see Mark Dubowitz and Ray Takeyh, "Labeling Iran's Revolutionary Guard," *Foreign Affairs*, March 6, 2017, https://www.foreignaffairs.com/articles/iran/2017-03-06/labeling-irans-revolutionary-guard. See also the State Department's description of the Order at https://www.state.gov/j/ct/rls/other/des/122570.htm

[24] Afshon Ostovar, *Vanguard of the Imam: Religion, Politics, and Iran's Revolutionary Guards* (New York: Oxford University Press, 2016).

Even as the United States engages more in the Middle East, it must also prevent allies from engaging in self-defeating behavior that gives Iran, Sunni jihadists, and other hostile actors opportunities. Saudi Arabia and other states must decrease their anti-Shi'a rhetoric and otherwise be willing to deescalate sectarian tension in order to improve relations with the Iraqi government and to take the wind out of the sails of the Islamic State and similar groups. The Saudi Arabian and Emirati intervention in Yemen has made the civil war there worse, given the Al Qaeda affiliate there far more power, and created an opportunity for Iran to expand its influence.[25] Pushing allies to negotiate and end the war will create opportunities to reduce ties between the Houthis and Iran as well as set back Al Qaeda.

Just as Iran faces limits on its power, so too does the United States face limits in its ability to reduce Iran's influence in the Middle East. The JCPOA, for all its faults, is better than any current alternatives. If the U.S. unilaterally abrogates the agreement, it is not likely that U.S. allies would curtail their economic ties to Iran or otherwise follow the U.S. lead. The situation would be far worse than it was before the JCPOA was signed. In addition, Iranian leaders who had championed the deal would fear losing domestic support and would be more likely to embrace hardline policies abroad. The United States, with its troop presence in Afghanistan, Iraq, and Syria, is highly vulnerable to Iranian proxy attacks and must recognize that escalation on the U.S. side can be met with escalation from Tehran.

An effective policy against Iran will also require a sustained and steady U.S. commitment. Inconsistent rhetoric, bombast, and efforts to score points to domestic audiences at the expense of Muslims will hinder U.S. efforts to build an anti-Iran alliance, among other costs. Similarly, anti-Iran rhetoric that is not tied to actual policies and events on the group will make Iran more likely to work with anti-American local groups. Unless the administration is more careful in its rhetoric, allies and adversaries alike are more likely to see the United States as unreliable or to simply ignore signals they do not like, leading to misperceptions that could backfire on the United States.

Finally, the Trump administration must set a realistic bar for success. Tehran's strategic options and desire to shape the Middle East to its liking will drive it to continue to work with a range of militant and terrorist groups and selectively use violence. Better U.S. policy can reduce the scope and scale of Iran's hostile activities but not end them altogether.

---

[25] International Crisis Group, "Yemen's al-Qaeda: Expanding the Base," February 2, 2017, https://www.crisisgroup.org/middle-east-north-africa/gulf-and-arabian-peninsula/yemen/174-yemen-s-al-qaeda-expanding-base.

Mr. Poe. And I thank all of you for your testimony. I will recognize myself for some questions.

I have introduced H.R. 478, the IRGC Terrorist Sanctions Act, and it would designate the IRGC for its terrorist activity under Executive Order 13224.

I want to ask each of you if you support that concept or you don't. And it is either a yes or a no.

Mr. Berman?

Mr. Berman. I do, sir.

Mr. Poe. Dr. Takeyh?

Mr. Takeyh. Yes, sir.

Mr. Poe. And Dr. Byman?

Mr. Byman. Yes, sir.

Mr. Poe. There are many things that I would like to go into, but let me just start with the first one.

Mr. Berman, you mentioned that the United States needs to develop a better relationship with the Iranian people, letting them understand that it is the regime that we don't support, but we support the people of Iran to be able to have self-determination to rule their own country and not the mullahs. Can you expound on how we could do that?

Mr. Berman. I can try, sir.

I think that a relatively underutilized tool that the United States has at its disposal is our ability to bypass the regime and communicate directly to the Iranian people through mechanisms like The Voice of America's Persian News Network and other broadcasting tools. And, here, what we say is as important as how loud we say it.

Programming that emphasizes the endemic corruption within the regime; that elevates the plight of individual political prisoners that are being maligned by the regime; that demonstrates to the Iranian people that, despite the economic benefits of the JCPOA, there has been no trickle-down effect that have benefited the ordinary Iranians. All of those things, I think, would help diminish the credibility of the Iranian regime, elevate America's standing in the eyes of the Iranian people, and really, I think, amplify all of the other elements of the Trump administration's strategy as it begins to be formed.

Mr. Poe. So if I understand you correctly, we should do everything we can to let the world and the Iranian people know that we support them in changing the regime in a peaceful way, that should be the U.S. policy as opposed to ultimate conflict, militarily, with Iran. Is that a fair statement?

Mr. Berman. Yes, sir. Yes, sir.

Mr. Poe. All of you mentioned Assad and also mentioned Iraq. What is Syria's relationship to Iran? Is it a puppet state? Same question about Iraq: Is Iraq becoming a puppet state of Iran? How would you characterize that relationship with Iran and those two countries?

Mr. Berman, you first

Mr. Berman. Absolutely. I will go very quickly, and I will allow my colleagues to step in.

I think it is necessary to think about Syria in the context of what it does for Iran, both as a strategic partner and as a buffer state.

Syria is part of that access of resistance that Iranian officials continually talk about withstanding pressure from the west, from the United States, and from Israel. Syria is a very important link in that access because of the land bridge that it provides to Iran's chief terrorist proxy, Hezbollah, in Lebanon. And the idea of a Syria that is no longer managed by a compliant partner, that is Balkanized or is subverted by a radical Sunni group, is anathema to Iran's long-term strategic interests, which goes a long way toward explaining why Iran has sunk so much blood and treasure into preserving the current status quo in Syria.

Mr. POE. Dr. Takeyh?

Mr. TAKEYH. I would agree with that on Syria.

I would actually suggest that—I wouldn't characterize Iraq as a state that today is a subsidiary of Iran. I think Iraqis don't want to be proxies of Iran. Iraq has institutions. It has some sort of a democratic structure, highly imperfect. And there is a lot of discussion nowadays about pushing back on Iran in the region.

I think the place that one can do so, perhaps as effectively as elsewhere, would be in Iraq, because Iraq has a history of being the seat of civilization as opposed to being a subsidiary of a Persian empire. And I do think Iraqi politicians, really across the board, would like to be emancipated from the Iranian influence. There are a lot of reasons they are not. They are not welcome—Iraq is not welcome in the council of Sunni Arab powers. That is something the United States can work on. And gradual integration of Iraq as a Shia state in a Sunni Arab—emphasizing their ethnic identity. So I think Iraq is a place where it is struggling to be free of Iran. But it——

Mr. POE. Let me ask you this last question.

And, Dr. Byman, you can give me your answer in writing. United States presence in Iraq, should it remain about the same? Should we ratchet up, militarily, our presence? Or should we just leave Iraq? Three options.

Mr. TAKEYH. I would imagine there has to be an enhanced military presence, but also an enhanced civilian presence in terms of Iraqi ministries, bureaucracy, and rehabilitating the institution. There has to be a greater degree of American presence, military as well as the civilian counterparts.

Mr. POE. Thank you.

The Chair will yield time to the gentleman from Massachusetts, Mr. Keating.

Mr. KEATING. Thank you, Mr. Chairman.

I think everyone, almost universally, whether they favored or didn't favor the JCPOA, acknowledged that they were about 8 to 12 weeks away from having a nuclear weapon. That was pretty well understood at that time. So as we are talking about a rejuvenated Iran, in all likelihood, we would be sitting here, in the absence of that agreement, having an Iran that had nuclear weapons. How could that not improve their influence and their malign activities coming from a strong point of having nuclear weapons to begin with? We are learning in North Korea how difficult that is.

Mr. Byman?

Mr. BYMAN. Mr. Keating, I favored the nuclear deal for exactly that reason. There are plenty of flaws with it, and we could spend more than this hearing pointing them out. But there aren't particularly good alternatives. And Iran without a nuclear weapon or Iran with a delayed nuclear weapon is better than Iran with a nuclear weapon right now.

Mr. KEATING. Thank you. That is where I—there were flaws. But you can't ignore that reality. As a matter of fact, Mr. Berman mentioned the Trump administration is embedded with this. They are not any more embedded than when the President said, on day one, he would tear up the agreement.

So what happened since the election?

Mr. BERMAN. Well, sir, I think it is one thing entirely to talk about tearing up the deal on day one as part of a stump speech during the campaign season. It is another thing entirely to recognize that, even though the JCPOA is an executive agreement and therefore can be terminated at the leisure of the next executive, it is actually a multilateral pact, and, therefore, the United States walking away from the JCPOA could end up in a situation where American leverage, notwithstanding, the JCPOA remains——

Mr. KEATING. Wouldn't that have been the case just at the time of the signing? It is all clear that the other participants in our coalition of sanctions—people, countries putting sanctions on Iran, they were ready to walk away then. And then we would have had the U.S., by itself, in Iran with a bomb. But that is just, I think, the real reason that tearing it up day one didn't occur, not because it was embedded.

But another question I have too, again, Mr. Berman. You said that it is the last 8 years that there has been a situation where Iran has advanced and gone through, implying that it was just under the Obama administration that that occurred. Nothing happened under the Bush administration? They weren't moving forward to its nuclear weapons and that capability? Nothing happened during that stage?

Mr. BERMAN. No. Sir, to clarify my point, I mentioned the two terms of the Obama administration in the context of America changing its relationship with the Iranian people directly. I think if you track the change in official rhetoric during the course of President Obama's two terms—and you can see that, for example, manifested in the annual New Year's greetings that every President since Gerald Ford has issued to the Iranian people on March 20th of every year. What you see is a trajectory that begins with communications to the Iranian people.

Mr. KEATING. Well, if I could interrupt. You know, we all know that security officials in the U.S. say they give Christmas greetings when they are making phone calls. But let me just put that in the context of saying, there was a progression of nuclear development during that year.

You know, I think we have to get, as much as we can, beyond the partisanship here, and that is the reason I pointed to those questions. These issues are far too important, and that is why I focused on that. But I must say that I favor too very strong sanctions in this area. And we can do that with no interference whatsoever with the agreement. There is plenty of options for the U.S., and I support them, because of Iran's military ballistic testing, ballistic missile testing, because of their human rights positions and actions, and because they are an exporter and enabler of terrorism through the whole region.

So I think we could do that. There is plenty of areas of agreement in that respect. So I want to thank you all for doing this and just say, on this important issue that we all agree is a central issue to our security, the extent that we move away from branding political partisan actions, we will all be stronger.

I yield back.

Mr. POE. The Chair recognizes the gentleman from California, Colonel Cook.

Mr. COOK. Thank you very much, Mr. Chair.

Dr. Takeyh, I wanted to ask you—I want to shift gears a little bit.

Saudi Arabia, since we are on the subject of nuclear weapons, there was a lot of speculation about the fact that with this agreement, that Saudi Arabia would unilaterally purchase or develop a nuclear device, because they are the, at least in recent years, the traditional enemy.

Do you have any comments on that in terms—I know it is hypothetical, but there was quite a bit of talk about it at the time.

Mr. TAKEYH. I think there were many things wrong with the Iranian JCPOA nuclear agreement. It is a flawed agreement. But I was never persuaded entirely of the cascade effect. Namely, that other countries would seek to emulate that capability. For one thing, I don't think the Saudis have this scientific foundation or a cadre to be able to, at this point, man an indigenous atomic nuclear program.

Mr. COOK. How about a purchase from a country like Pakistan?

Mr. TAKEYH. I am not a Pakistan expert. But should Pakistan have sold a nuclear weapon to Saudi Arabia, it would be the first state to actually transfer nuclear weapons to another state. Without precedent. Now, if anybody can break precedent, it is the Pakistanis. I just don't know enough about Pakistan. Every time I would ask somebody who knows something about Pakistan, they will say they would do it.

Mr. COOK. Okay. Can I switch gears a little bit?

I want to talk about Bahrain, and the number of Shia residents there, and the influence of Iran on a pivotal country. Obviously, that is where our fleet is and everything like that. Do you have any comments on that? Because the Bahrain is involved in the war in Yemen, and which I am sure is, you know, as part of the Saudi coalition, and whether that is the next, if you will, in this domino effect of countries that Iran has supported.

Mr. TAKEYH. In the Gulf today, Bahrain remains a country that has been most vulnerable to Iranian subversion, and the activity of Iran subversion in Bahrain utilizing the Shia population is increasing to the extent of, I think, even dispatching arms. So Bahrain is becoming a specific target of Iran's, as they will say, malign activities, more so than, I think, other places in the Gulf, simply because there have been disturbances there in the aftermath of 2011, and Iran always tries to fish in muddy waters. So I think you are seeing a greater degree of subversive participation in Bahrain at this point.

Mr. COOK. Okay. And last question or issue I want to talk—and, Mr. Berman, I haven't picked on you. And I apologize. But the war in Yemen, and particularly, once again, the Saudi investment, in terms of that escalating, this is tremendous consequences for the Red Sea and the closure of the Suez. If that continues, with an escalation, how do you think that could play out in terms of involvement of those countries in the region and the United States?

Mr. BERMAN. I will attempt very briefly.

I think that the proper lens through which to view what is happening in Yemen—and, incidentally, it is worth noting that Yemen is in the throws of three separate security crises, not simply the civil war. However, the instability that is localized there now has the potential to have a very large catalytic effect on the safety and security of energy shipping through the Bab al-Mandab and other strategic waterways. And it is also, I think, correct to view what is happening in Yemen as, at least in part, a proxy battle between Iranian-supported rebels on the one hand, and the Saudi state, and the Gulf monarchy, the Sunni Gulf monarchies, on the other.

There is, I think, a very high potential for escalation because of these characteristics, and it is a crisis that I think the Unites States needs to navigate very carefully.

Mr. COOK. Thank you, very much. I yield back.

Mr. POE. I thank the gentleman.

The Chair recognizes the gentlelady from Nevada, Ms. Titus.

Ms. TITUS. Thank you, Mr. Chairman.

You know, we have just heard for the last few days a lot about the President's trip to the Middle East and to Israel. And so we have heard him talk about cooperation and new directions and all of that. And that is why I would just point out, again, that while your testimony is very interesting, and I thank you for being here, it is not all that helpful moving forward. It is good analysis, but we really need to hear from members of the administration to put some meat on the bones here. Just what are the plans? What are the details? What do they have in mind going forward with this new direction?

I would just ask you, quickly, Mr. Berman, you mentioned several times the need to reach out beyond the government to the people of Iran. I wonder if you know what the new budget does to Voice of America, for example.

Mr. BERMAN. Ma'am, I do. I think the conversation about the current shape and content of U.S. broadcasting toward Iran specifically is a work in progress. I can divulge—I have on public forums—that my organization, the American Foreign Policy Council, has been asked to do an independent third-party review of content relating to Persian-language broadcasting, and I will reserve all judgment until the findings of that study come back. But I would hope that those findings will have an impact upon how the administration sees the utility of strategic communication.

Ms. TITUS. I hope so too, because at a time when apparently we need it even more, it is being cut by about 9 percent. So let's just get that on the record.

I will now ask you, Dr. Byman. In your written statement, you note that—and I will quote you, if you don't mind: "The new initiative or form of pressure is going to require our allies. Economic pressure requires support from European and Asian allies, while military and diplomatic pressure requires Middle Eastern help as well."

I would like to go back to the point that our ranking member was making about the nuclear agreement. Another statement that came out of the travels of the President from Saudi Arabia was that, and I quote again: "Iran's interference poses a threat to the security of the region and the world, and the nuclear agreement with Iran needs to be reexamined and some of its clauses."

This was a statement coming from the U.S. and Saudi Arabia. Now, Saudi Arabia wasn't part of that original agreement. So it is kind of confusing. And on the other hand, we are hearing that Iran lived up to its agreement. Now we are hearing we need a new direction involving Saudi Arabia.

Could you tell us what you think the other members of the original agreement are going to think about opening up again and looking at some of these provisions and working with people who weren't even part of the original agreement?

Mr. BYMAN. As you know, the agreement required painful and also painstaking diplomacy. And I think many countries walked away, not completely satisfied, but at least getting some sense of what they were hoping for. The problem with opening this up again is that it looks like it is the United States that is doing it when, at the same time, the United States is certifying that Iran has lived up to its side of the bargain in letter. Not always in spirit but in letter.

And, as a result, many of our allies would be skeptical of this, and I think we would end up worse off than we were in 2011, that the economic pressure that was brought to bear in 2011 would be very difficult to rebuild because the problem would be seen as emanating from Washington rather than from Tehran.

My hope would be that we could build economic pressure on other issues, not the nuclear issue, but terrorism, such as the subject of this hearing, for exactly that reason. I think Iran should be pushed to move away from much of its nasty activity, but doing so, on the nuclear agreement, without a clear violation from Iran, in my mind, would be a mistake.

Ms. TITUS. So you don't think that, say, Russia or China or some of the European countries would think this was a good idea?

Mr. BYMAN. I hate to invoke Russia or China, because I think they would happily rush in to exploit any sense of a U.S. misstep or a weakness. But I would even say real allies, allies in Europe, for example, most of them would think it was a mistake.

Ms. TITUS. Thank you. I yield back.

Mr. POE. I thank the gentlelady.

The Chair recognizes the gentleman from Pennsylvania, Mr. Perry.

Mr. PERRY. Good afternoon, gentlemen.

Thank you, Chairman.

Mr. Berman, looking for, and I think you kind of enumerated some in your testimony, but I would like to go back through it a little bit. Iran's use of the funds released from the JCPOA to increase funding to terrorist organizations and activities. If we could kind of delve into that a little bit, the amount, to who, and how that is verified.

Mr. BERMAN. Thank you, sir. And I am happy to provide more details. I have written about it and I have documented it elsewhere. So please forgive if I provide—if my incomplete memory——

Mr. PERRY. An overview will be good.

Mr. BERMAN. The Congressional Research Service in July 2015, about 2 or 3 weeks after the passage of the JCPOA, was asked by the office of Congressman Mark Kirk—of Senator Mark Kirk to outline what it believed was the scope of Iranian, then-sanctioned Iran, its funding, the scope of its funding for international terrorism. At that time, what was returned by the CRS was not a figure, but it was a range. It was a range between $3½ billion and $16 billion annually, at a time when Iran was still constrained by multilateral sanctions. And that range encompassed everything from between $100 million and $200 million annually to Hezbollah to up to $6 billion annually, at that time, for support for the Assad regime in terms of troops and materiel, to several dozens of millions of dollars for Iraqi militias. There were sort of very clear sort of line items that were enumerated in that report. And I am happy to make that available to you.

I think sort of the takeaway from the time that has elapsed since has been that while a full snapshot of how much Iran is spending on this portfolio is still incomplete, at least in the Open Source, it is clear from certain data points in the Open Source Press, for example, that Iran has ratcheted up this financial activity with regard to Hamas, with regard to Hezbollah, in a way that is very detrimental to regional security because it expands the threat capabilities.

Mr. PERRY. So at what level? How do we determine at what level? And can you, with any confidence, conclude, for instance, missile technology Tomas, is directly attributable to the money that was received from Iran, from the United States as a result of the JCPOA?

Mr. BERMAN. Sir, I think it would be very hard to point to a smoking gun in terms of direct transfer as a result of the JCPOA. What I would note, at least for the purposes of this hearing, is the overall expansion of available funds that are fungible that Iran can use for a variety of——

Mr. PERRY. We all get that, obviously. So currently, only the IRGC Quds force is designated by the Treasury for its terrorist activities. And I am thinking, you know, Mr. Mast, my time in Iraq where Iran, it was directly attributed, their use and manufacture of EFPs, explosive form penetrators, which is a cheap manned sabot round, goes right through an engine block, and certainly a human is—you can understand the devastation. I am wondering how we are going to—how we are going to sanction the broader IRGC under the requirements designated in the Executive Order 13224 and if we want to. But, first of all, I think we should. But maybe you have a different opinion. But how do we justify that? I mean, when we know these things are—you know, the IRGC is a big operation in Iran, controlling most of the activities of the country in a meaningful sense. So how do we get to that?

Mr. BERMAN. Well, sir, in sort of—in the very short time I have allotted, I would point out two things. First of all, there is a policy goal of preventing a full normalization of trade with Iran that the administration has articulated. And in this context, the IRGC is very much low-hanging fruit. They control a third or more of Iran's national economy. They have controlling interests in the telecom sector, in the construction sector, and various other aspects of Iran's economy, and, therefore, a designation would have a chilling effect on—can be expected to have a chilling effect on foreign countries and companies that are involved in those sectors.

Mr. PERRY. So what would be the downside and how do you—can we justify it currently? I know we got 30 seconds. Can we justify it currently and is there a downside?

Mr. BERMAN. I think there is a downside. There is always a downside in these sort of designations. I believe that it could create not insubstantial trade disruptions between the United States and countries that are heavily leveraged in the Iranian market. I think this is not an insurmountable obstacle as well. And I think what we will find is that the lion's share of countries and companies that are involved in the Iranian market are much more heavily leveraged in the American market, and we can force them——

Mr. PERRY. I am not worried about the leveraging.

Mr. Chairman, with your indulgence—the justification, can there be any justification under the current circumstances to designate the greater IRGC?

Mr. BERMAN. You mean a precipitating event, sir?

Mr. PERRY. How do we know where they are spending the money? I mean, how do you prove the justification for designating them? If we haven't done it already, what has changed?

Mr. BERMAN. Well, the lack of a designation up until this point, sir, I would argue is actually a failure of policy, and it reflects sort of a desire to turn a blind eye to the——

Mr. PERRY. Okay. So you are saying we currently have the justification.

Thank you, Mr. Chairman. I yield.

Mr. BERMAN. Yes, sir.

Mr. POE. The Chair recognizes the gentlelady from California, Mrs. Torres.

Mrs. TORRES. Thank you very much, Mr. Chairman. And thank you to our panel for being here.

How could the Trump administration policies toward Russia, in recent statements during his trip to the Middle East about Iran, affect the United States' ability to pursue its objectives in curbing Iran's destructive influence in the region?

Mr. BYMAN. It is a very big question. So I will say perhaps the most important first step is to restore confidence of U.S. allies in U.S. leadership. And that requires a sense that the United States is going to hear their concerns, but also that the United States is going to become and stay a major player in the Middle East. And that requires military presence. It also requires a political presence. It requires high-level engagement, and it requires almost constant lower-level engagement as well. And maintaining those ties, making sure allies are on the same page, making sure we have a plan, that is going to be necessary. That is hard for any administration. And I hope that the Trump administration can use any momentum from the recent trip to try to restore and build that coalition, and then develop the capacity within Washington to carry that energy forward.

Mrs. TORRES. Lower-level engagement as in?

Mr. BYMAN. We need deputy assistant secretaries. We need people who are political figures throughout the administration who are often the counterparts. Any President, no matter how energetic, cannot handle every aspect of diplomacy 24 hours a day. Secretary of State cannot do so. And we need experts and advisors and mid-level officials, and that is vital to any administration's success.

Mrs. TORRES. I was hoping you would say that. Thank you.

This subcommittee has previously heard testimony regarding the role of Iran and Russia in supporting the Taliban and the Shiite militias. How do their shared security interests impede U.S. objectives in the region and what options does the U.S. have in confronting those efforts?

Mr. TAKEYH. This is one of the more curious aspects of Iran's policy in a sense that it is willing to, at times, align itself with even radical Sunni groups. There are some indications of some level of relationship with al-Qaeda. There is always a relationship with some members or aspects of Taliban, and Russia has been doing the same thing.

In this sense, there is a measure of amorality in terms of Iran's policy, particularly as it looks east in terms of Afghanistan. One of the ways of combatting that, as Judge Poe has his own legislation on the revolutionary guards, one of the ways we principally over the time have tried to impose penalties and costs on Iran is through economic measures. Whether they have been successful or not is hard to say. But that economic leverage, I think, is important to suggest, that coercive economic leverage is attenuated because of JCPOA. There are barriers and obstacles to that. So JCPOA is a nuclear agreement, but its restrictions also affect the progress of the United States in exercising the economic leverage tool that historically has deployed.

Mrs. TORRES. Anyone else?

Mr. BERMAN. If I could, ma'am. I would point out, this, to me, is one of the central questions in our conversation about Russia and sort of where Russia fits. And I think there has been quite a learning process that the new White House has gone through.

In the early days of the Trump administration, there was a lot of talk about whether it was possible to flip Russia on Iran, whether it was possible to get Russia, with a more specific relationship overall, to get Moscow to cooperate better on Tehran. But what we have discovered is that this is actually much harder than it looks, for a whole host of very practical reasons.

Russia needs Iranian assistance and support in order to preserve a long-term presence in Syria, for forced projection in the Middle East. Russia, whose own economy is not doing well, needs those tens of billions of dollars of arms deals that has now concluded with Iran. And for these and other reasons, it is, I think, a little bit facile to think about the fact that Russia, with enough inducements, with enough carrots, will actually play ball on Iran. I think we need to start thinking more creatively about what tools of leverage we have that can separate the Russians from the Iranians in what is manifestly a very robust——

Mrs. TORRES. I want to get a last quick question in there. What cooperation, if any, is there between Iran and North Korea regarding ballistic missile development?

Mr. BERMAN. I have 10 seconds, so I will have to be very brief. I would point out that the strategic relationship dates back to the late 1980s, but it extends beyond ballistic missiles. Every single nuclear test that the North Korean regime has carried out in the past decade has had observers, Iranian engineers as observers. And this——

Mrs. TORRES. On the ground?

Mr. BERMAN. On the ground. And this speaks to a larger, deeper, and more nefarious strategic relationship, not only on ballistic missiles, but on other strategic programs as well.

Mrs. TORRES. Mr. Chairman, thank you for the 17 seconds.

Mr. POE. You are welcome.

I know the State Department is looking for deputy secretaries. I think maybe three are right here sitting in front of us, though. You don't have to comment on that.

The Chair recognizes the gentleman from Virginia, Mr. Garrett.

Mr. GARRETT. Thank you, Mr. Chairman.

Sort of trying to wrap my brain around this is something, because, you know, I have only been here for a few months, and my background is as a company grade military officer and a prosecutor. And yet I look at the JCPOA, which at the risk of getting myself in trouble, I refer to as the JCPOS, and I wonder who wrote it. And what I mean by that is, if you look at U.N. Resolution 1929 that was controlling in 2010, the wording of the document read: Iran shall not undertake any activity related to ballistic missiles capable of—right? And then under the JCPOA we were handed language: Iran is called upon not to undertake any activities related to the development of ballistic missiles.

Dramatic pause for effect. Right? You don't have to be that good a lawyer and certainly not that experienced a legislator to understand the difference between "may" and "shall" or "shall not" versus "is called upon not to."

Mr. Berman, at what possible point did any individual commissioned by the United States of America and the P5+1 think this wording made sense, and could you please shed some light on to why?

Mr. BERMAN. Sir, I can't. And I say this advisably as a not very good lawyer who is recovering currently. I would point out that that language is dispositive. And what you have seen—and it is not only on the ballistic missile portfolio but on other aspects of multilateral pressure against Iran, where we have seen a watering down in the service of the nuclear agreement. And this is the only explanation I have for it, that in the service, in the hope that we could delay and potentially later derail Iran's nuclear program, we were willing to roll back the language, the compulsory nature of our international restrictions so far.

As we have seen, I think this was a bargain that hasn't manifested itself as a good one, and I think we are now sort of trying to make up lost ground as a result.

Mr. GARRETT. So, Mr. Byman, you testified that Iran has lived up to its side of the bargain, and this is a quote: "In a letter if not in the spirit."

I am not aware of your educational background, but does it shock you that when the previous oversight of Iran, as it related to U.N. Resolution 1929 was "shall not undertake," and the JCPOA— JCPOS—JCPOA says, "is called upon not to," does it shock you that Iran has engaged in ballistic missile activity?

Mr. BYMAN. Not at all, sir.

Mr. GARRETT. And does anybody at the table know who it was that we empowered as a Nation and where they went to law school, who thought that this language is a good idea? Right?

Mr. Chairman, if you will indulge me for a moment, it is not just about the procurement of a nuclear device. Right? A nuclear device needs a delivery mechanism. And so while you might take some short-term windows and say we have moved that back as we watched North Korea right now, not in the SCIF, we also know that there is miniaturization and mating a nuclear device to a delivery mechanism.

And so you contemplate the terms of breakout. Is it not possible that Iran is angling toward a creep-out knowing that the mechanisms for delivery are being enhanced under our very nose by a language that we allowed, that someone was either criminally negligent or was aware of the intent, and that we are going to have a creep-out scenario where Iran not only has a nuclear weapon but also their delivery mechanism by which to essentially hold hostage the entire region if not the world?

Mr. Takeyh.

Mr. TAKEYH. A nuclear weapon requires a number of things. It requires ability to enrich uranium with dispatch. Iran is currently developing the capacity with the advancement of this high-level velocity centrifuges, which are permissible by JCPOA. It requires ability to design—weaponization design. That is impossible to detect. Weaponization design could be a room in an office somewhere, so I imagine that is taking place.

Third is projectiles to deliver that missile, and that is also excluded from the agreement, and therefore, they are developing those ballistic missiles. So the triad of a nuclear weapon is being developed right now.

Mr. GARRETT. I have a finite amount of time. I respect the answer, and I will come back to you. But essentially, it wasn't excluded from the agreement. We included—that is the delivery mechanism development. We included words in the JCPOA that at least politicians could come back to the American and global consuming public and go, oh, look, we have called upon them not to undertake the development, right, whereas we all understand "may" versus "shall" versus "called upon not to," right?

So we didn't deny anything other than agreeing to a reduction of the number of centrifuges and eliminating plutonium centrifuges for a period of time. Am I correct?

Mr. TAKEYH. The plutonium capability has, I think, been foreclosed but not the enrichment capacity—enrichment capability. And you are right. In the Resolution 1929, it was impermissible for

Iran to develop ballistic missiles. That language has obviously been attenuated, as you know.

Mr. GARRETT. Thank you.

And thank you, Mr. Chairman.

Mr. POE. I thank the gentleman.

The Chair recognizes the gentleman from Illinois, Mr. Schneider.

Mr. SCHNEIDER. Thank you.

And I apologize, I am in another hearing where we are having a vote, so if I jump up abruptly, please don't take offense. But thank you for your testimony. Thank you for your work. I was not able to be here for your testimony here, but I have studied your submitted testimony carefully, and I very much appreciate it.

I think, Dr. Takeyh, you describe in your—you close in your remarks that, in the end, the nuclear agreement offered Iran all that it wanted and go on to identify that. I think that, for me, at the time was one of my concerns with the agreement, as well as the matter of time. But we are stuck with this agreement now. We are where we are. And I am sure you have talked about it in previous discussion, the need to enforce this agreement, enforce it to its letter.

Mr. Berman, in your testimony, you talk about ensuring compliance and akin to the question. There is a great deal—you say there is a great deal that must be done in this regard. Could you highlight some of the specifics of what you see being absolutely necessary and what the Congress can do to move this forward to make sure that we absolutely lock down this agreement for the time we have it to make sure Iran doesn't get any closer to a nuclear weapon?

Mr. BERMAN. Sir, I can hazard sort of the start of a guess. I think there is a more fulsome response that requires some study. But I would point out that the current regime—monitoring regime structure that exists under the JCPOA is inadequate for a couple reasons. First of all, it is not fully sourced in the sense that the facilities that the United States Government believes are Iranian nuclear facilities are not completely covered by the inspections regime that is baked into the JCPOA.

There are additional facilities that need to be looked at. There are many facilities that are co-located with military bases that are overseen by the Revolutionary Guard Corps, which are of specific concern.

And there is also a—there have been limitations that have been imposed by the Iranian regime on free, unfettered access for the inspectors that do exist in their coming, going to these facilities.

All of these ambiguities, as a start, should be assessed and discussed in order to determine whether or not we have adequate confidence that with this limited regime we can see everything there is to see.

Mr. SCHNEIDER. Great. Thank you.

Dr. Byman—and I promise, Dr. Takeyh, I am going to come to you as well.

But, Dr. Byman, you say that the administration should, and I will quote you, "lay down clear red lines regarding Iran's support for militant groups," and other things. What are the red lines you see? Again, what can Congress do to help state those, articulate them as clearly as possible but make sure that if those lines are crossed, there is articulated consequences as well?

Mr. BYMAN. To say some that I hope are obvious and therefore could gather support across a wide spectrum of Americans would be any targeting, of course, of the U.S. homeland or any targeting of American assets overseas.

And one thing we haven't done in the past is we have frequently ignored plots and focused on actual attacks, which I understand the political logic of that, but that is crazy, because some of the attacks could have easily happened. We were just a little lucky and a little skillful. And so that is where I put the emphasis. Obviously, any transfer of unconventional weapons to a terrorist group should be red lined.

The thing I would emphasize, though, is this is something Congress should be heavily involved in because we have to show that this will span administrations; that regardless of who is in the White House, that the United States will act to stop those.

Mr. SCHNEIDER. Thank you. I can't agree more with what you just said. And one of my issues with the JCPOA is that it is not just administrations but generations. And my concern with this 15-year term, and we see with the recent election, is that the people who signed this deal on the Iranian side have every expectation that they will be in power when the deal expires and can just wait it out.

Dr. Takeyh, I want to come back to you. I want to give you the last word. You very, I think, cogently said—and, again, I am going to quote: "A regime is dangerous to U.S. interests as the Islamic Republic requires a comprehensive strategy to counter it."

Hopefully, we can see a comprehensive strategy coming from the administration in conjunction with working with Congress. But are there things that you believe have to be—absolutely necessary—be a part of that comprehensive strategy, and, again, what can Congress do to further that?

Mr. TAKEYH. Well, one of the things—one of the things I would say is—I think it has been mentioned before—is the rebuilding of the alliances in the Middle East. Those alliances for a variety of reasons have been battered in the past few years, and once again, rekindling that particular capability of those.

I would say in terms of hemming Iran's influence, as I mentioned before, I think Iraq is a place where we can more aggressively and effectively push back on Iran. That essentially is a very important battleground for Iran because it is far more important to their national interests and security objectives than I think Syria is. And it is the place where the United States has a greater degree of assets.

Finally, I will say, I continue to stress that it is important to put economic pressure on Iran. But, again, I have to emphasize, that ability to impose economic pressure to some extent is weakened by JCPOA and its provisions of economic relief that have to come about, particularly in the realm of financial institutions. Because one of the things we found out, maybe belatedly, in between 2011 and the aftermath, is that the United States has the ability to segregate Iran from the global financial institutions. And that has a real effect on its domestic economy and its ability to project power, subsidize militias, and everything.

And I think that particular instrument is now largely—not entirely, but to some extent weakened by JCPOA, particularly in terms of central bank sanctions and so on.

Mr. SCHNEIDER. Right. No, I think we are limited. I hope that as a body, as was stated, that we can make it clear to Iran that it is the policy of our Nation, of this Congress, not just now, not just for the term of the agreement but forever that this regime will never get a nuclear weapon.

So, again, I thank the witnesses for their testimony, and I yield back my time.

Mr. POE. I thank the gentleman from Illinois.

And I thank all three of you all for being here today, for your excellent testimony. There may be more questions that members have. They will put them in writing, and they will submit them to the Chair, and we will submit them to you all for quick answers.

So thank you very much. The subcommittee is adjourned.

[Whereupon, at 3:19 p.m., the subcommittee was adjourned.]

APPENDIX

MATERIAL SUBMITTED FOR THE RECORD

SUBCOMMITTEE HEARING NOTICE
COMMITTEE ON FOREIGN AFFAIRS
U.S. HOUSE OF REPRESENTATIVES
WASHINGTON, DC 20515-6128

Subcommittee on Terrorism, Nonproliferation, and Trade
Ted Poe (R-TX), Chairman

TO: **MEMBERS OF THE COMMITTEE ON FOREIGN AFFAIRS**

You are respectfully requested to attend an OPEN hearing of the Committee on Foreign Affairs, to be held by the Subcommittee on Terrorism, Nonproliferation, and Trade in Room 2172 of the Rayburn House Office Building (and available live on the Committee website at http://www.ForeignAffairs.house.gov):

DATE: Wednesday, May 24, 2017

TIME: 2:00 p.m.

SUBJECT: Nuclear Deal Fallout: The Global Threat of Iran

WITNESSES: Mr. Ilan Berman
                    Senior Vice President
                    American Foreign Policy Council

                    Ray Takeyh, Ph.D.
                    Hasib J. Sabbagh Senior Fellow for Middle East Studies
                    Council on Foreign Relations

                    Daniel L. Byman, Ph.D.
                    Senior Fellow
                    Center for Middle East Policy
                    Brookings Institution

By Direction of the Chairman

The Committee on Foreign Affairs seeks to make its facilities accessible to persons with disabilities. If you are in need of special accommodations, please call 202/225-5021 at least four business days in advance of the event, whenever practicable. Questions with regard to special accommodations in general (including availability of Committee materials in alternative formats and assistive listening devices) may be directed to the Committee.

COMMITTEE ON FOREIGN AFFAIRS

MINUTES OF SUBCOMMITTEE ON _____ *Terrorism, Nonproliferation, and Trade* _____ HEARING

Day __*Wednesday*__ Date _____ *May 24, 2017* _____ Room _____ *2172* _____

Starting Time ___*2:09 p.m.*___ Ending Time ___*3:19 p.m.*___

Recesses _____ (____ to ____) (____ to ____) (____ to ____) (____ to ____) (____ to ____) (____ to ____)

Presiding Member(s)

Chairman Ted Poe

Check all of the following that apply:

Open Session ☑
Executive (closed) Session ☐
Televised ☑

Electronically Recorded (taped) ☑
Stenographic Record ☑

TITLE OF HEARING:

"Nuclear Deal Fallout: The Global Threat of Iran"

SUBCOMMITTEE MEMBERS PRESENT:

Reps. Poe, Keating, Cook, Boyle, Perry, Titus, Zeldin, Torres, Mast, Schneider, Garrett

NON-SUBCOMMITTEE MEMBERS PRESENT: *(Mark with an * if they are not members of full committee.)*

Rohrabacher

HEARING WITNESSES: Same as meeting notice attached? Yes ☑ **No** ☐
(If "no", please list below and include title, agency, department, or organization.)

STATEMENTS FOR THE RECORD: *(List any statements submitted for the record.)*

SFR submitted by Rep. Brad Schneider
QFR submitted by Ranking Member Bill Keating for Mr. Ilan Berman

TIME SCHEDULED TO RECONVENE _____
or
TIME ADJOURNED ___*3:19 p.m.*___

Subcommittee Staff Associate

**Terrorism, Nonproliferation, and Trade
Subcommittee Hearing
Nuclear Deal Fallout: The Global Threat of Iran
May 24, 2017**

**Rep. Brad Schneider
Opening Remarks (1 minute)**

Thank you, Chairman Poe and Ranking Member Keating, for holding this important hearing today. I look forward to hearing from our witnesses and participating in what I imagine will be a fruitful discussion.

I have been working to prevent Iran from acquiring a nuclear weapon for almost two decades. While I did not support the nuclear deal with Iran, now that it is in force, we must ensure Iran strictly adheres to the agreement and is held accountable for any and all violations.

Iran has not changed its malign behavior since the JCPOA. It is still a top state sponsor of terrorism, supports terrorist proxies, and continues to be a destabilizing force in the region. Iran also continues to work on and test its ballistic missile program. I support additional sanctions on Iran outside the purview of the JCPOA in response to these unacceptable actions.

There is no bigger threat to the existence of our greatest ally, Israel, than Iran. But, this is not just a problem for Israel. This is a global problem that every nation should be worried about. I look forward to continuing to work with my colleagues on both sides of the aisle to ensure Iran never acquires a nuclear weapon – not now, not during the life of the JCPOA, not ever.

Question for the Record for Mr. Ilan Berman
submitted by Ranking Member William R. Keating
Terrorism, Nonproliferation, and Trade Subcommittee

Expand on your comments about inadequate inspections under the JCPOA and your proposal to demand access to additional nuclear facilities not currently being monitored under the JCPOA.

The current inspections regime enumerated under the terms of the JCPOA is not comprehensive, and fails to provide the international community with sufficient oversight over the length and breadth of the Iranian national nuclear enterprise.

- Under the terms of the JCPOA, "routine inspections" carried out by the International Atomic Energy Agency (IAEA) are limited to sites that have been formally declared by Iran (rather than all sites believed to be involved in nuclear work). Moreover, the Islamic Republic has the right, as a practical matter, to refuse access to other facilities on its territory that are suspected of being involved in nuclear work, at least temporarily.
- Pursuant to its obligations to the IAEA, the Iranian regime is required to proactively notify the agency of the design and construction of new nuclear sites. However, no independent means of verifying possible nuclear-related construction currently exists, and the international community is reliant on the Iranian regime to promptly and fully disclose its new nuclear work—something that Iran has repeatedly failed to do in the past.
- The protocol governing access to suspicious or undeclared sites under the JCPOA is both extensive and laborious. It potentially entails formal notification to Iran from the IAEA, a period of clarification and negotiation, and then—if necessary—a "dispute resolution" process involving both Iran and the P5+1 powers.[1] This process is highly advantageous to the Iranian regime should it seek to obscure relevant data and processes relating to its nuclear work. It is also far short of the concept of all-access inspections originally propounded by proponents of the deal.
- To supplement physical inspections, the JCPOA authorizes IAEA inspectors to use "modern technologies" (such as automated data collection) to carry out monitoring of Iran's nuclear facilities. However, prominent experts have raised concerns that the Iranian regime, itself a sophisticated cyber power, could "game" such virtual access in order to project an erroneous or fabricated picture of the state of its nuclear program.[2]
- Finally, even if it is granted full access to the entire Iranian nuclear enterprise, the IAEA currently lacks the manpower to police it properly. According to the Institute for Science & International Security, a respected nonproliferation think tank, there are in excess of thirty separate sites within the Islamic Republic believed to be involved in one way or another in the country's nuclear program.[3] However, the IAEA has only between 130 and 150 designated inspectors dealing with Iran, and that membership in that contingent is limited to nations that have

full diplomatic relations with Iran (thus expressly excluding American specialists from directly monitoring Iranian facilities).[4]

In sum, the provisions enumerated under the JCPOA are simply not sufficient to ensure accurate and comprehensive monitoring of the totality of Iran's nuclear work. Much more must be done in order for the United States and its allies to gain greater confidence that the Iranian regime is strictly complying with its obligations to the international community with regard to its nuclear program.

---

[1] For a succinct summary, see Iran Watch, "How Will Inspections Work in Iran under the Nuclear Deal?" July 14, 2015, http://www.iranwatch.org/our-publications/policy-briefs/how-will-inspections-work-iran-under-nuclear-deal.

[2] See, for example, Samantha Ravich, remarks at the American Foreign Policy Council's conference on "Iran After the Nuclear Deal," Washington, DC, April 4, 2016. A summary of Dr. Ravich's remarks can be found here: http://www.afpc.org/event_listings/viewConference/3159.

[3] Institute for Science & International Security, "Nuclear Iran: Nuclear Sites," n.d., http://www.isisnucleariran.org/sites/alpha/.

[4] Iran Watch, "How Will Inspections Work in Iran under the Nuclear Deal?"